BEACH
HUT
PEOPLE

*NANCY
STEVENSON*

BEACH HUT PEOPLE

NANCY STEVENSON

Publishing Household

BEACH HUT PEOPLE

First published in Great Britain in 2023 by Publishing Household.
Imprint of The Nose, 28 Newgate Street,
Walton-on-the-Naze, Essex, CO14 8AL

thenose.org

The right of Nancy Stevenson to be identified as the author
of this work has been asserted by her in accordance with
Copyright, Designs and Patents Act 1988

Every effort has been made to trace copyright holders and obtain
their permission for the use of copyright material. The publisher
apologises for any errors or omissions and would be grateful
if notified of any corrections that should be incorporated
in future reprints or editions of this book.

British Library Cataloguing-in-Publication Data

ISBN 978-1-7393567-0-5

Typeset in Miller Text 10.75pt

Design by Claire Mason
Printed and bound in Great Britain at Clays Ltd

To Charlie and Elliot

CONTENTS

Southcliff, Walton

1 — STARTING

It's morning at low tide and we are wandering along the water's edge on the beach at Walton-on-the-Naze (Walton) in Essex. I am daydreaming as I look up at the cluster of small huts, sardined together on the slope and casually snap photos with my phone:

"Charlie, why would anyone want to own a beach hut?"

I'm still walking, not really paying attention. My words merge with the sounds of the waves. You pause and then as you carefully compose your photo, exclaim that they look lovely. I stop and follow your gaze. You have a point. There is something charming about this beach hut village with its pastel hues. Something that is quintessentially English seaside and evokes childhood memories of days at the beach. I continue...

"They look nice enough. But who would want to own
a wooden shed on a small patch of crumbling slope by
the sea?"

You shrug, take your photograph, and we walk on in silence.
My question remains unanswered.

OK, so it is a small question, about the minutia of
people's lives. It is local, personal and probably doesn't
deserve much scrutiny, but the question resurfaces every
time I walk past the huts. I speak to friends and neighbours
and discover that I am surrounded by people who love
them. I feel like the only one who doesn't get the punch line
of a joke. It is not a good feeling. Clearly, I have a lot to learn
and I spend days walking along the promenade peering
into huts and glimpsing excerpts of other people's lives.
I note down beach hut names, take photographs and read
local history books, but can find nothing that gives me an
insight into the experiences, motivations and feelings of the
people who choose to spend time in beach huts. No amount
of reading, imagining or watching answers my question.
I realise that if I want to understand the people who inhabit
beach huts, I need to talk to them. I start to collect and
record their beach hut stories on my walks along the
seafront between Walton and Frinton-on-Sea (Frinton).
Gathering this information is not a chore as I love meeting
new people. The rest of my family are more reserved and
regularly joke that I can't be left alone for five minutes
without striking up a conversation with a 'random stranger'.

The book provides an excuse to talk to strar̶
embrace my 'superpower' as I embark on a missiᴏ
out more about people I don't know.

In this book I share the stories of the people who guide
me in my journey from puzzled outsider to someone who is
starting to appreciate the pleasures of a day at the beach
hut.

IGNORANCE

My beach hut journey begins on that morning walk and
stems from that unanswered question:

"Why would anyone want to own a beach hut?"

At the outset I have limited experience. I have never owned
or rented a beach hut myself, but have visited them with
friends for picnics or barbecues. Spending a day in a
brightly coloured hut sits well within my imagination of
a perfect day at the beach, however, my experiences prior
to starting this book are not positive. My first beach hut
experience occurs on The Leas when friends invite us to
join them for lunch in a hut that they have rented for a
week. The hut has long views of the beach, and is set up
high on a grassy slope. It is a chilly, grey August day and the
wind whistles in through the front door and hatch. It starts
to drizzle after about an hour and we bring damp clothes,
sandy towels and fold-up chairs into the hut. We drink tea
and eat gritty sandwiches in the cramped, cold, dank,
squalid interior. We haven't brought enough warm clothes

and we huddle together shivering. This beach hut is miserable, provides no refuge, and we wonder when it will be polite to leave. Children whine and shiver, adults are irritable and bored.

My second experience is on High Wall in Frinton in another weekly rental hut. This one is in a less exposed location, set back in the second row with no view of the sea. It is a warm and sunny day and the hut provides some basic comforts for our beach experience. These include a battered collection of old deckchairs, several cheap white plastic chairs, an ageing gas hob, a kettle, a few old mugs and some beach toys. It also provides a private place to change and to get out of the sun. We have a marvellous day — children play happily, chatting as they build an elaborate sand city and splash around in the sea — adults play, talk, read, swim and drink endless cups of tea. We enjoy the most wonderful time together but spend almost no time in the hut which is dark and musty.

We can't see the hut from the beach and feel that we should lock it up when no one is inside. The locking and unlocking process is repeated many times throughout the day and requires both dexterity and patience to release the big, rusty, awkward padlock. The beach hut is the hub for our gathering but it feels like a responsibility. The wooden steps are steep and rickety, the gas burners are initially difficult to light, then whoosh into high flame. The smell of gas permeates the hut and throughout the day we make repeated checks to see whether there is a leak. We seem to be constantly carrying things in and out, up the steps and back down. At the end of the day we clean, wipe down and sweep a space that seems to have become remarkably dirty in the context of its limited use. My question resurfaces:

'Why would anyone want to own a beach hut?'

It is separate from the beach and everything about it seems to detach me from the very place I want to be and the things I want to do — namely sitting and playing on the sand, paddling in the sea and enjoying the multiple pleasures of the beach. We enter a time-warp, with the women retiring to the hut to make tea, prepare sandwiches and wash the crockery. The men engage in the more masculine activities, setting up the gas supply and struggling with the rusty lock. Women chat and men dig; women sweep and men carry.

A beach hut seems to impose a structure upon the wonderful lack of structure that I crave from a day at the beach. That sense of lack of purpose, of doing whatever comes, responding to the weather and the tide. Just enjoying the contrasting sensations of the sand. Fine dry sand above the high tide line, pillow soft and perfect for relaxation and sunbathing; complemented by gently ridged, hard damp sand that emerges as the tide ebbs. A solid foundation for sandcastles, a place for activity and ball games. A good day on the beach encompasses people, lots of people — time spent sitting in close proximity to strangers. Random conversations in a shifting, shared space. On the beach people are in constant motion — streaming down the hill in the morning, setting up their camps and then reworking them in response to changes in the weather and the tide creeping back up the beach. A good day on the beach encompasses both intense activity and relaxation, an opportunity to be outside, to paddle or bathe in the sea and to interact with the people around.

As I start this book my own experiences leave me unconvinced. I am frustrated by my lack of understanding, my inability to appreciate the simple pleasures of a day at a beach hut and am determined to learn more.

BECOMING A BEACH HUT PERSON

What sort of knowledge do I need to understand beach huts? I realise that my lack of childhood experience means I don't have the nuanced understanding and nostalgic recollections which might enable me to fully appreciate a day at the hut. I start to talk to people and I am introduced to the idea of 'beach hut people'. The first time I hear the term is when I speak to Lynette and her daughter Rebecca. Lynette grew up in New Zealand and says that people don't have beach huts there. She remembers that as a child she saw small off-grid cabins in natural places or by the coast but she never stayed in one. Lynette moved to the UK but did not visit a beach hut until her daughter bought one. Rebecca explains:

> "We are not beach hut people. We are not from beach hut families. I can't imagine my dad coming. It is not

his world at all. I have no childhood memories of huts".

Despite her lack of childhood experiences Lynette falls in love with the idea of having a hut on her first visit. She buys one almost straight away, then another, and then decides to move to Walton. She has evolved into a fully-fledged beach hutter and has over a decade of experiences and memories of days spent at the hut with friends and family.

As I start to find out more about these 'beach hut people' the idea of a book takes shape. People share their recollections with me and I learn about the processes, practices and pleasures associated with owning a hut. I am welcomed in, shown around and learn more about provenance of the items on display in their huts. I find out about collections of shells, postcards, pictures, photographs and vintage crockery. People share tales about childhood visits with family and friends and their memories of special occasions celebrated at the hut. Many older hut owners tell me about the 'heyday' of the beach huts at Walton and Frinton, identifying this as the period between the mid 1940s to the late 1970s. Some come from families who have owned huts for generations, and others recall their parents renting the same hut each year during the summer holidays when they were children. People share tales of beach hut routines in the past, summer friendships, big Sunday dinners cooked in the hut and communal games on the beach. Rose coloured memories of endless sunny days, a sense of freedom and of childhood summers full of fun.

STORIES TOLD IN TURBULENT TIMES

The stories for this book have been collected during a very
challenging time. In 2019, the practice of visiting the huts
appears to be in decline and many remain shuttered
throughout the summer. People tell me that their children
and grandchildren, prefer to travel overseas for holidays
and are not particularly interested in a day at the hut. They
share their concerns that their beach hut has less appeal
than in the past and many doubt that their family beach hut
tradition will be embraced by future generations.

Then in 2020, the Coronavirus Pandemic leads to
restrictions and a major shift in people's behaviour and
travel patterns. The dynamic of both resorts, and of the
beach huts changes. With international travel restricted,
many people choose to holiday closer to home and flock
towards British beaches. The beach hut once again
becomes desirable, providing a refuge not just from the
uncertainties of the British weather but also from proximity
to others when the beach becomes crowded.

During the summer of 2020 I pause. It is not possible
to speak to people in their huts as rules about social
distancing are still in place and arranging interviews
outside is difficult because of a temporary ban on people
sitting outside their huts on the promenade. However,
I continue to make repeated visits to the beach and to jot
down my observations about the changes in occupancy
rates, hut names and a trend towards refurbishing huts.
Beach hut rentals are booming and are marketed through

online platforms and also through an informal market supported by notices on the front of huts, and word-of-mouth. I watch as the rental offer becomes more sophisticated with a growing array of themed beach huts, and the provision of additional amenities such as towels, bottles of prosecco, and services such as cream teas delivered to the hut during the afternoon. As prices start to rise, many long-term hut owners decide it is time to 'cash-in' and recoup on their unexpectedly lucrative investment.

In 2021, the growing popularity of beach huts is covered in the national press and Radio 4 with several short interviews with hut owners in Frinton and Walton — a good news story in difficult times. Beach huts are back in fashion and more huts are refurbished with nostalgic or quirky designs that quickly become a part of the illustrated life stories of Instagram influencers. The beach hut is all the rage, bang on trend and prices continue to rise as more people want to own huts for themselves or to rent out to others. As lockdown restrictions start to ease in May 2021, people settle into their huts and I start to collect more stories.

SHARING BEACH HUT STORIES

This book is based on conversations with 60 people who own or regularly visit beach huts. All except one of the stories are gathered in or just outside beach huts. Initially I approach people randomly but as the project progresses,

The Parsons Family, Eastcliff, 1967

I am introduced to their beach hut neighbours and other friends with huts who are happy to talk to me and share their recollections.

In the following chapters I share tales about people's experiences and memories of beach huts and explore feelings evoked by a day at the hut. These tales take us beyond the materiality of the hut — past its scant wooden structure. They uncover intangible aspects associated with time spent in a beach hut which create memories that stir people's emotions and generates positive feelings. As I meet more people, I realise that these insubstantial structures are full of meaning. Sarah captures this when she refers to her hut as:

> "our shed by the sea" but then goes on to explain "but it is so much more than that. It's an escape, it reminds me of my childhood. It is just idyllic".

I discover that these sheds by the sea provide the backdrop to countless imagined, lived and remembered lovely days. Sometimes they are joyful places where people can have fun with friends and family; other times they provide space be alone, to reflect and just gaze at the vastness of sea and sky. They can provide a sanctuary — a place to tuck away from the cloud bursts, strong winds, blazing sun, and to escape from other people and the stresses of everyday life. Beach huts are bursting with imagination, hope, dreams, and memories.

Frinton, 1927

2 — PEOPLE

I look at local history books and see old pictures of bathing machines, tents, and huts but can find little information about the people who actually choose to own or stay in them. In *Low Country: Brexit on the Essex Coast*, Tom Bolton recounts his walks along the Essex coastline and talks about its settlements, people, topography and its history. As he sets off towards the Naze beach, he notices "the village of beach huts inhabited by friendly pensioners" (2018:215). I wonder about his description. How can he have missed the families, and the children? I guess that he visited on a school day and out of season? If he had come during the summer holidays or at the weekend he would have come across younger hut owners and noticed that many huts are occupied by families and groups of young people.

It is difficult to label beach hut people as being 'this' or being 'that'. They share a common interest and congregate in a specific place, spending time at the beach, in a hut and in close proximity to others. But a closer look reveals many differences — the people I meet come from different walks of life, and they are not all elderly. Being a beach hut person is a state of mind. It is possible to become one after just a few hours but for many it takes weeks, years or generations to become a fully-fledged beach hutter.

My storytellers are adults, aged between 20 and 80. Without exception, they are convivial and friendly when I approach them to ask them about their beach hut experiences. I am invited to sit with them and often offered a cup of tea and a slice of cake. Lynette invites me for breakfast in the hut and we spend a couple of hours eating, talking and looking out towards the sea.

Most people that I meet travel less than an hour to visit their hut and many come from nearby towns like Colchester, Ipswich, Sudbury and neighbouring villages in North Essex. The few people from further away are from London or Hertfordshire, and usually have a holiday home or caravan close by. Whilst most people are happy for me to use their names in the book, some opt for anonymity and so in a few cases I have created fictional names. I have chosen English names which are common in the UK. This is no accident and reflects the cultural background of the people who commonly visit the huts, and the make-up of the area more generally. While day trippers create a more cosmopolitan feel when evening comes the resorts once again become more culturally uniform places.

I wonder how to introduce these beach hut people without overwhelming you. Imagine that we are walking along the promenade together. It's a sunny day and there are dozens of families setting up in the huts. I recognise some people who have contributed to the book, and as we approach I will tell you a little more about them. We will pause, say hello, exchange pleasantries and then walk on to meet a few more people. You probably won't remember their names but the next time you are here you'll recognise them. Perhaps you'll wave, or chat for a few moments and it doesn't matter that neither of you can recollect the other's name. Our walk starts in Walton close to the pier at Southcliff where we meet some of the people whose stories are included in the book.

RUTH, CLIFFORD AND RICHARD

When I first meet Ruth and Clifford in 2019, they are reading and sunbathing outside their front row hut, glamourous and glistening in the sun. They are frequent visitors and I have often noticed them during my walks along the beach. Inimitable and stylish, they arrive at the start of each season in a Rolls Royce, exuding a deep tanned, manicured, and carefully coiffed film star glamour from another age and another place — more St Tropez than Walton. Their flawless and distinctive attire is matched by an immaculate beach hut with a pink and white interior.

I am not surprised when I find an image of them online by Martin Parr. It was taken in 2017, included in his exhibition *The Great British Seaside* at the National Maritime Museum in 2018. A few months after our conversation I find another photograph online taken by Niall McDiarmid in 2019. In my imagination their flawlessness is accompanied by frostiness, and so while I have been fascinated by them for years, I have never actually talked to them. The beach hut book finally gives me a reason and the courage to strike up a conversation. My imagination has not served me well and I discover that they are really friendly. Ruth invites me to join them, shows me family pictures inside the beach hut and shares her family's beach hut history:

> "We have had a hut since 1953 when my grandfather bought it after the first lot of floods. We have always had a hut in this place but over the years we have had to replace it. As the family increased, we bought more and so we can have the whole family down. Our family has three huts now. They are all close by. One is just there and one at the back".

When we finish our conversation Ruth introduces us to Richard, her beach hut neighbour. Richard is sitting outside his hut called *E' solo un caponnone* with his partner Pam. His family have had beach huts for over 70 years and he has countless childhood memories of being at the hut. Ruth and Richard have been neighbours since childhood and used to play on the beach together. Richard recalls:

"My dad bought a beach hut when I was a baby in the 1940s. It was a lot different then, there was only one row at the front here, and maybe just a few at the back, and the huts ended at the corner there. We lost one in the floods in 1953 and got another one more or less straight away. Dad had number 72 and he had that until we were all grown up. And there was a time when we didn't own a beach hut because I was away and my brothers and sisters were away. In 1984 I came back from Scotland and my sister said let's get a beach hut together and we bought this one. We used to have 72 and this is number 79".

Although Richard lives quite close by he seldom visits his hut and prefers to travel around the country in his campervan. The day we meet is a special occasion as Pam's children and grandchildren are visiting from Hong Kong and we watch them playing in the shallow water. Later, they join us outside the hut and tell me that they have never been to a beach hut before. They are really enjoying their day but think the English coast is chilly and the grandchildren are dressed in wet suits. They tell me that they love the beach hut because it provides them with some indoor space so that they can warm-up after a paddle in the North Sea.

We say goodbye to Ruth, Clifford and Richard and continue on our walk around the headland to the huts on The Leas.

ANNA, GLENN AND PIPPA

Anna is renovating *Pearl*, her new family hut. She regularly posts pictures on Instagram illustrating their progress, or sharing images of items that she has bought for the hut and their days at the beach. She normally visits with her husband, Glenn; her daughter, Pippa, and the family dog Poppy. They bought their hut in 2021, and prior to that regularly rented a neighbouring hut with their friends. Anna is a teacher and works part-time which means that she sometimes visits on her own to progress with painting and renovation works. When I first meet her, she is on the beach with her close friend and their two girls and tells me:

"I grew up by the beach. I am from a fishing family from Mersea. My grandfather, my dad and his brothers are all fishermen. My grandmother and her sisters bought a beach hut at West Mersea and we still have it. The way the family has always run it is that everyone helps pay for the ground rent, and everyone has a key and you can go and use it as you wish. We use it sometimes, but it is not our hut.

We fell in love with this beach when my friend hired a hut in Frinton about five years ago. Here it is very shallow so it is just so child friendly. When we come here it feels like a treat. And because I grew up in Mersea visiting the hut there didn't feel like a treat. This is our hut and we can put a stamp on it. This will be the place where we make memories".

SUE, MARTIN AND SARAH

Sue, Martin and Sarah own adjacent beach huts called *Katrina &* and *The Waves*. When I first meet them in 2019, Sue has just opened her beach hut and is awaiting the arrival of friends. Sarah and Martin are chatting to her as they sit outside the hut next door. They have become friends through their regular trips to the beach hut and went to Womad (a world music festival) together in 2018. Both Sue and Sarah visited huts when they were children in the 1970s. Sarah and Martin live just outside Colchester and travel to their hut by train at the weekends throughout the summer. Sue lives in London but visits regularly throughout the year as she has a second home in Frinton. She shares her childhood recollections:

> "My dad worked at Ford. We were quite poor but he put a lot of money into having a hut in Walton. So, when I was born, we already had a hut down there and we had it until it burnt down when I was in my late 20s early 30s. When I had children of my own, I bought one here, knocked it down and put a new one on it. We have had this one for about 15 years".

OLIVIA AND TERRY

Olivia and Terry are sitting in the sun on the paved area outside their hut. They have just finished lunch and are enjoying a cup of tea together. I meet them in May 2021, early in the season but they visit regularly and both are

already tanned. Their main home is on the outskirts
of London in Woodford Green and they have a flat that
overlooks the beach and is a five-minute walk from their
hut. They bought their beach hut two years ago and prior
to that rented the one next door for the whole of August
every summer for a decade. They have recently retired and
I see them at their hut throughout the summer often
entertaining family and friends. While they have only
owned a hut for a couple of years, they feel that beach
hutting is part of their family history. This feeling is
supported by dozens of family photographs taken at the
beach hut next door over the years.

Now that I have introduced a few people on The Leas we
will continue our walk towards the huts at High Wall.

JENNY GEOFF AND AMY

Jenny, Geoff and their daughter Amy have had a family hut
on High Wall for 15 years, but have been coming to Frinton
annually for over 25 years. They live about an hour away
and rent a flat in Frinton for a week each summer. Before
they bought a hut, they used to rent one each year so that
they could spend every day of their Frinton holiday on the
beach. Amy says that she has always loved visiting the
family hut, even during her teenage years. This year she is
really busy as she is studying at University, and working
part-time in a pub. Visiting the hut is particularly enjoyable
because it is one of the few places where she can disconnect
from her phone which provides her with some quiet time:

"If I want to use my phone I have to walk to the end of the beach. It is great to disconnect and just to enjoy being here. To have a cup of tea, sit, and relax".

The family bought their own hut when Jenny's grandmother died and her mum inherited some money. Three generations of the family share the hut, sometimes visiting together and sometimes alone or with friends. Amy loves coming for family days or larger gatherings of friends and family. Jenny particularly enjoys spending time at the hut with girlfriends while Geoff often likes to come alone or with the dog.

MARY

Mary is sitting outside her hut alone watching the sea. She lives in Frinton and visits regularly. She has owned two huts and tells me that she and her husband previously bought one on the front when their boys were little. They used to visit regularly for breakfasts, dinner parties, sports nights and church events. Then as the boys grew older, the family bought a small fishing boat and started to spend a lot of time on the water. They decided to sell the hut because they no longer used it. Then years later, after her boys had left home, she was unwell and some friends lent her their hut while she was convalescing. She really enjoyed the experience and when her mum died, she inherited some money and decided to use it to buy another hut. She visits regularly throughout the year and while she still entertains friends and family at her hut, she particularly enjoys visiting on her own. She uses it as a base for daily beach walks with her dog and a place to just watch the sea and reflect.

On our imagined walk I have introduced you to just a few of the people who shared their stories for this book. I hope I have given you a sense of the variety of people who like to spend time at their beach huts.

BEACH HUT COMMUNITY

People who own and regularly visit their huts consider themselves to be part of a beach hut community. Common interests, shared experiences and the physical proximity to hut neighbours combine to foster many long-term friendships. Some people tell me there are several distinct beach hut communities in the different locations on this part of the coast (See map in Chapter 3 *PLACE* p.28). I hear that the 'posh' huts are located in Frinton and the 'poshest' are those at The Walings close to the golf club. Sally has a hut on The Leas which she calls "the middle-class bit". She jokes:

> "If you go towards Frinton and the more expensive huts, they are more likely to be drinking Chablis. If you go towards Walton, they are more likely to be drinking Watney's Pale Ale. Walton has always has been a bit more crowded... everyone crowds in and sometimes it feels like a bit like a cockney knees-up around there.

They have the pier and the candyfloss and we haven't got anything and that is great".

Kevin and Sophie have two rental huts on Southcliff and visit regularly throughout the year when their huts are not hired out. They enjoy being part of the Walton beach hut community:

> "It is such a nice place and it always seems more friendly and down to earth than Frinton".

Emma's family live locally and have owned a beach hut on Eastcliff for many years. She explains that there is a strong sense of community on this stretch of beach even though there are lots of rentals. This is because many of the weekly renters come back year after year. They are not close to the station which means that there are fewer day trippers that on some other parts of the beach.

The huts in Frinton cost more than those in Walton but there appear to be few differences in terms of the behaviour or friendliness of hut owners along this stretch of coast. When I first meet Robert and Lindsey they have owned a hut on High Wall for just two days and are settling in:

> "We have noticed how friendly people are. Everyone talks to you as you walk along and there is a community. People give advice and share their top-tips".

Margaret lives locally and for many years she rented on High Wall. She now owns a hut on The Leas and tells me that she still socialises with her beach hut neighbours in both locations:

> "There is a bit of a community and so obviously you get to know everybody just in your little group wherever your hut is. I am still friendly with the our beach hut neighbours from the hut in Queens Road. Our beach hut friends are casual. Generally, we don't socialise or agree to meet when we are not at the beach but we always have a chat if they are here".

All along the beach, people tell me that their beach hut is a social space, a place to be friendly and to natter. When I speak to Ruth on Southcliff, she tells me that chatting is one of the pleasures of spending a day at her hut:

> "There are quite a few people who live down here who we see whenever we come. And then there are the regulars who always walk by and then come and chat. We always talk to people. We know more people here than we do at home!"

Ruth and Richard think there was a stronger sense of community in the past. They reminisce about camaraderie in bygone times when holiday makers would rent the same hut every year and get to know the local families who owned huts. Richard talks about longstanding friendships with people from other huts:

"I've got people coming next week who live in Derby now. I have known Roger for years. He has come down since he was two years old. When his family first came my dad was still around and they rented the beach hut next to us. We used to sit outside shelling peas and doing the potatoes and we got to know them because this little boy used to come over and help my dad. At the end of the week, they had to be out of their beach hut by Saturday lunch time because they were renting it. They were staying until the next day and my dad said 'why don't you come to our hut'. And from that time on they came and stayed at ours. He came down for years and he brought his two boys down and so on. And those two boys have grown up now but he has met someone else and has a boy who is about 6 and he is coming down. Must be 50 years we have known them and they have come down and stayed at our house.

You develop friends here. I have known Ruth for years and as a boy I have thrown water at her when she was sunbathing and she got up and chased me and stuff. So, I know her family, and there used to be loads of them. They were the ones that we used to get together with, and we would have a barbecues and parties".

Almost everyone I speak to supports the idea of rentals, however there are some concerns about the impact of day rentals on the beach hut community. This is particularly true of Southcliff where there are often different people coming in each day and these huts can attract very large groups who hire them for family events and parties. Ruth explains:

"There are more people who are buying them up and renting them out on a daily rental basis. So, there is less of a community because they are people who will be here today and you might never see them again and there will be another lot tomorrow. Whereas in the past you saw the same people. I think we are losing the community spirit here".

Several people share stories about unruly behaviour when huts are rented to large groups of people. Debbie says:

"Sometimes you get really noisy families and there are a lot of people and it is a bit rough".

Olivia tells me:

"In the summer, sometimes they get huge parties of people on Southcliff — and they come with radios and it can be a bit intimidating".

Despite these concerns most people still identify a sense of community with their beach hut neighbours. This sense is created informally through regular conversation, or as people help one-another out by opening rusty padlocks or assisting with the heavy storm doors. Community relations are formalised and enhanced by the beach hut associations at Walton and Frinton. Members volunteer and regularly patrol a stretch of huts to check for damage and liaise with neighbours if there are any problems. People tell me that the patrols are invaluable as they are immediately notified if their huts are damaged by the weather or vandals. Beach hut people look out for one another and that creates a strong sense of being part of a community.

SLOWING DOWN

Before I started collecting information for this book I regularly walked along beach between Walton and Frinton. I often said hello to people in their huts, but I was always on the move and never engaged in conversations with them. Years as an outsider, looking, wondering, imagining, but not actually asking. Now that I have learned to slow down and ask questions, I am amazed at how friendly beach hut people are. Everyone is eager to chat, to share their experiences and their sense of good fortune at being able to spend time in a beach hut.

The introductions in this chapter give you a sense of the people who shared their stories and of the beach hut communities in Walton and Frinton. You will meet them again as I start to explore different aspects and experiences of owning and spending time at a beach hut. In the next chapters you I will introduce more people I encounter on my journey towards becoming a beach person.

HIPKINS
BEACH

EASTCLIFF

WALTON ON THE NAZE

SOUTHCLIFF

THE LEAS

FRINTON ON SEA

HIGH WALL

THE
NORTH
SEA

LOW WALL

THE WALINGS

BEACH HUT LOCATIONS

3 — PLACE

Before I share more beach hut stories, let me describe the place. Frinton and Walton are small resort towns located in the parish of Tendring, North Essex. Each has a railway station and a distinct separate centre, but over the years their hinterlands have merged. While the boundary is delineated on maps, and is clear in the minds of many residents, to the casual eye the threshold of each place is indistinct. On the seafront there is a continuous promenade and my conversations with beach hut owners reveal some confusion about the edge of one place and the beginning of the other.

The histories of the two places are distinct yet intertwined and are explored in local history books such as *Frinton and Walton Through Time* by Michael Rouse, *Frinton and Walton: A Pictorial History* by Norman Jacobs,

Pushed to the Edge: A History of the Naze and Walton Hall by Ben Eagle and *The Naze: Walton on the Naze* by Steven Walker. In writing this book, I aim to add another layer to these local histories by sharing stories and experiences from the beach hut community.

Frinton has a reputation for being up-market, and for many years resisted providing some of the services traditionally associated with English seaside resorts. There was no fish and chip take-away until the 1990s and no pub until 2000. There are ongoing battles with ice cream sellers, who are not allowed to trade on the seafront and in 2020/2021, furore when a couple start to sell ice creams and refreshments first from a bike and then from a van. The row is reported in the local and national press. In 2020, the Daily Mail quotes local councillor Nick Turner:

> "This town is not a seaside resort, it's a town that welcomes visitors who come here and treat it like the locals do and become part of that environment, not hostile to it.
>
> If you want to bring the family here to enjoy the sun, sea and sand, fine. If you want the razzmatazz go to Clacton or Walton because those places are geared up to that and that's what they do".

The idea that Frinton "is not a seaside resort" is repeated by Terry Allan the Deputy Mayor in an interview with the Clacton and Frinton Gazette. In 2021, an article in the Times says that Frinton is 'Tourism Shy' and the Telegraph

calls it a 'notoriously stubborn Essex town'. I am unable to
find detailed tourism figures for the two resorts, but the
Tourism Strategy 2021–2026 for Tendring, shows that in
2018 the value of tourism was over £400 million and visitor
numbers were 3,986,000. It is difficult to understand the
idea that Walton is a tourist resort and Frinton isn't. In both
places there are shops that sell buckets and spades, gift
shops, tea-rooms, fish and chip takeaways, cafes, licenced
restaurants, bars and pubs. Both are crowded with visitors
in the school holidays and on sunny weekends and there is
tourist accommodation in hotels, guest houses, B&Bs,
short-term rentals and Airbnb.

Walton has a broader range of facilities with three
caravan sites, refreshment kiosks on the seafront, the pier
and pubs/bars with a view of the sea. Its pier is the third
longest in the UK, and like many other piers around the
country its fortunes are in flux as I collect stories for this
book. In 2019, the landward end of the pier is covered and
houses a bowling alley, fairground rides, an amusement
arcade and a café/bar. Beyond the fairground it is open
and stretches out into the sea, providing a place for people
to fish or walk out to see the lifeboat stationed near the end.
In 2021, the pier looks neglected, its facilities are much
reduced with the bowling alley gone and large indoor café/
bar closed. Its open part is in disrepair and part way along
it has been cordoned off which means that it is no longer
possible to walk out to view the lifeboat. The pier becomes
an eerie place in the evenings and out of season when

bored local youth gather to talk, smoke, throw chips at one another and clamber on rides which have closed for the evening. There are two newly installed fairground catering kiosks on the windswept forecourt just outside the pier entrance. In the summer these provide fish and chips and hamburgers to be consumed on the picnic tables just outside the arcade or taken back to the huts or onto the beach. There is a sense of dereliction when the kiosks are shut, a detritus of food wrappers swirl around the forecourt. That winter the pier closes, is boarded up and is slowly refurbished. I watch and wait as windows are boxed in, internal partitions ripped out, old rides are packed up and transported from Essex to Barry Island Pleasure Park (a Gavin and Stacey moment in Walton's history!). In the summer of 2022, the pier reopens, nightclub dark with neon lights, a large arcade, new bowling alley, music and food. But in late 2022, as I finish editing this book the pier is only partially renovated. Beyond the arcade the old furniture is piled up high and much of the open part at the end is still in disrepair and inaccessible to the public.

Both resorts sit in Essex, a much-maligned county, its people caricatured in the 1980s and 1990s as Essex Man and Essex Woman — brash, blingy, money-driven, working-class Tories. Its proximity to London means that its beautiful coastline is often overlooked. People speed up the A12 for weekend breaks and summer holidays in Suffolk and Norfolk.

THE BEACH

People visit Frinton and Walton for the beach which is predominantly sand and gently slopes into the sea. At high tide in most places the beach is covered by water. Day trippers arrive, exclaim in disbelief, pause and check their phones. This is not the beach they were hoping to find, the one that they saw online or in pictures. The tide shapes a day on this beach and they must wait a while at the edge of the sea, relax, and watch as the beach re-emerges.

On the coast, the boundary between land and sea relentlessly shifts. The incoming tide encroaches, waves submerging land, and later ebbs away to expose a wide expanse of fine white sand, shells and a few pebbles. Every day this landscape is reworked by waves and tides. Somedays the sand is piled high, and others it is scooped back out to sea, revealing a bed of grey clay at the low water mark. The beach is a place of constant change, one day shrouded in seaweed and the next picked clean.

The beaches at Frinton and Walton are shaped both by nature and man. Moulded by breakwaters, wooden groynes, a grey concrete sea-wall and gabions filled with rock. The infrastructure at the front line in the ongoing battle to hold the edges of our tiny island in place. The sea defences are austere — the architecture of war. We battle as we attempt to defend ourselves against the encroaching sea. The sea dances around our defences, carving ever changing pools and channels in the sand, nibbling at concrete walls and then launching full attack on these austere enemies during

winter storms. *Time and tide wait for no man* — we forget
the lessons from King Canute as we endeavour to stop land
slumping seaward and beach migrating inward.

THE HUTS

The beach huts sit at the edge of this battlefield, nestled
into the grassy slope and facing out to sea. These painted
sheds with their pastel hues, bunting and whimsy are the
architecture of pleasure and play. They are designed to
support a day on these blustery North Sea beaches and
shape the social life of the resort, both reflecting and
reinforcing local culture and activities. In Walton, wooden
café kiosks sit, surrounded by huts on the promenade
selling ice creams, coffee, sandwiches, doughnuts, chips,
and buckets and spades. Sustenance for a day at the beach
and a destination for walkers throughout the year.

There are over 3,000 huts in Tendring, many of which are
located within these two resort towns. Huts ribbon along the
seafront in different configurations. At the southernmost tip
of Frinton Beach, The Walings, a single row of huts perch on
stilts above the beach in front of the sea wall. These huts have
raised decks that face out towards a low-lying golf course and
back windows overlooking the beach. Further to the North at
High Wall and The Leas, huts are generally one or two rows
deep and face out towards the sea. On the steep slope of
Southcliff at Walton, huts nestle together, five deep in some
places — a beach hut village. Then right next to the pier, a
new development of beach huts on private land. Smart new

The Walings, Frinton

pastel huts in an area with a 'no entry' sign on the gate by the promenade and a private carpark. The exclusivity of the 'gated' development is undermined by its density and thus the relatively modest space to sit outside.

Just North of the pier there is a stretch with no huts, the land becomes flatter, the beach backed by wall, road and buildings. Further on there are more huts set just above the beach backed by a low slope called Eastcliff. And finally, another cluster of huts are located on the slopes above Hipkin's beach. These are slightly larger and set on private land and this is the only place where overnight stays are permitted. Beyond Hipkin's beach is the Naze, designated as 'A Site of Special Scientific Interest' (SSSI), and where cliffs erode and crumble into the sea. Granite rocks form a partial defence encompassing a raised walkway, interpretation boards and a place to view the exposed and shifting cliffs. Here a beach of grey London clay is uncovered at low tide revealing treasure; fossilised shark teeth, wood, whale bone, pebbles and shells.

LOCATION

Beach hut location is important and has geographical and social dimensions. Everyone I meet explains why their hut's position is perfect for them, taking time to elucidate some of the benefits of their chosen site. There are varied perspectives about the desirable qualities of different places. Proximity to the pier is an attraction to some, providing a place for the kids to play and somewhere to visit when it is rainy. For others the pier is a noisy, crowded, expensive place and has little appeal. The desirable qualities of hut location are explored further below.

1. *Close to the access slope, the toilets and taps*
Proximity to the pathways and routes from the road, public toilets and water taps are generally considered to be desirable. At the huts on The Leas, Anne explains the advantages of being close to the vehicular access slope:

> "When our parents were in their nineties, we used to have a key to the gate and we could drive them down and drop them off here and then take the car back up. And then after grandma had died, grandad could come down in his wheelchair".

Emma's family hut was near to the road and the slope on Eastcliff and this enabled her grandparents to continue visiting as they got older and meant that her mum could still come when she was sick:

> "When my grandad was really old, he was in a care home at the Naze, and he liked to come down on his mobility scooter".

2. *On the less crowded parts of the beach*
At the huts on High Wall, people tell me that they prefer to be located away from the access routes and the toilets because the beaches in these areas are busier in the summer.

Maureen and Phillip live in Frinton in a flat that overlooks the sea and their beach hut is a five-minute walk from home:

> "We could have had one a bit closer to where we live but it is quieter here away from the pathways down the slope".

George and Catherine also chose to locate away from the pathways:

> "We are located a short distance away from the toilet blocks and pathways down. These two beaches are always fairly empty when the ones just at the end of the paths are very busy".

People tell me that the huts on The Leas are quieter because they are set back on a grassy slope in an area where the promenade is wide and the beaches less crowded. You met Olivia and Terry as we walked along the beach in Chapter 2, *PEOPLE*. They rented the same hut each August for ten years before they finally found one to buy in their favourite location. The hut they now own is on The Leas with long views of the beach and is next door to the one that the used to hire. They love its location because of its orientation and proximity to their flat. Terry explains:

> "We thought that this was the very best place to have a beach hut. It has the view, the grass slope in front and we are set on the South facing curve which means we get sun here for much longer in the evening. And so, when this one came up for sale, we decided to go for it".

3. *Located on the promenade*

Most people who are located on the promenade talk about the importance of being close to the beach and of being able to see the children when they are playing. Graham is on the northern end of High Wall. He lives close by and visits regularly on his own, and with three generations of his family. He explains that the location of his hut works particularly well when his family visits:

> "It is near to the toilets which is great for the kids when they come and it is straight on to the beach and you can see them playing there".

The joys of 'people watching' are mentioned in many conversations with people who are located on the promenade. Rebecca says that a front row hut combines:

> "All the loveliness of the beach, the friendliness of people chatting outside their huts and a space to watch the world go by".

4. *Set back from the promenade*

I meet some people who prefer their beach hut to be set back on the slope, especially on Southcliff where the promenade can become very busy during the summer. The huts further back are quieter, more sheltered and often have decks and a better view of the sea. Jemima lives locally and bought her beach hut in early 2020, at the end of the first lockdown. We meet in September 2020 on a sunny day and talk as we sit together on the large deck in front of her hut. She explains what she likes about being located in row C on Southcliff:

"I never wanted a beach hut on the promenade because it is noisy and it is busy. I love tourists but they walk up and down all day. You don't have any privacy and when the tide comes in you sit with lots of people. I wanted to be close to a dog friendly beach, the toilet and the tap, and to be able to walk to town and amenities. I realised that Frinton was ridiculously expensive and I always thought I would buy one of the ones near the pier on the corner because they are nice colours and are pretty. However, they have tiny decks with no barriers around the edge so your chair can easily fall off. The land is owned by a private company and the site fees and car park are expensive. I had not thought about Southcliff but then this one came up. I tentatively bought it overnight before I viewed it because it sounded like a good deal. And when I came here and saw that it was in the third row with nothing in front, I felt it had to be. I hadn't realised how lovely it was up here, the view here is uninterrupted. I had never thought about what view and privacy you get here which is second to none".

Lynette talks about one of her previous huts which was also in row C on Southcliff:

"There was a wide path in front of it. When you opened the storm shutters it had some old French doors that came out of an old summer house. It was just gorgeous because the whole front of the hut opened up. It was beautifully done inside and the view was fantastic as there was no row B at this part, so you got this fantastic view. It was like a horse with blinkers because you couldn't see all the other huts".

Martin tells me that he likes being located slightly up the grassy slope on The Leas:

"We have more of an elevated view here. We can look down over the beach and we have this large grass area outside the hut. When the tides in we can stay up here and sit out on the grass. Sounds seem to be amplified — the sea, the voices of children, the dogs. I sometimes just lay down and just listen to everyone on the beach".

Melanie likes to be tucked away in row B on Southcliff. partly for the view but also because she really notices the sounds of the beach in her hut:

"Although I am apart from it, I feel a part of it. I love the sound of the beach... it is like the sound of swimming pools, the sound of people being happy. You rarely hear a child cry... it is a place where children are really happy and they are just doing the things that children have done for generations".

5. *Proximity to the pier*
Some people talk about the advantages afforded by being

41

close to the pier in Walton, which offers amenities that they associate with a good day at the beach. Karen explains:

> "It's near enough to the pier for my grandchildren if they come down and want to go to the pier. There are amusements there, and a café and toilets and it is good to have those things close by".

Other people stress the importance of having a hut that is located away from the ice cream kiosks, the pier and the fish and chip shops. Both Sue and Emma like to be further away from the pier, partly because they think that area is crowded with day trippers and partly because they like their children playing on an uncommercialised beach and of them having fun without constantly wanting other things. Emma has three children and tells me that she does not want to have to spend a lot of money every time she visits her hut. She visits regularly but normally takes her own food and says that she only buys ice cream from the beach kiosks on special occasions.

6. *Located on a dog-friendly beach*

A dog-friendly beach is one of the essential criteria for many people when they choose the location of a hut. Many people talk about the pleasures of regularly bringing their dogs down to the beach. Graham visits nearly every day:

> "Often, I come on my own with the dog. I will have a walk and then the dog will sit in my lap and I will have a cup of coffee and do the crossword".

Many of the beach hut stories include tales about dogs enjoying a day at the beach. Fred's dog loves the beach:

> "We like to give her a walk when we get here. She is a greyhound and she goes berserk for 20 minutes and then she sleeps all day".

All the beach hut people I meet seem to like dogs. Even those who don't own them tell me that they enjoy watching other people's dogs running and playing on the beach.

IT'S ALL ABOUT THE BEACH

The one thing that all the hut owners agree upon is the importance of being located close to a sandy beach. Karen talks about the feel of the sand as the tide is going out which is: "kind to the feet, compacted, clean and nice". Kevin loves visiting at low tide: "when you have got acres and acres of beach". I realise I have something in common with the beach hutters — we all love this stretch of coastline and visit it regularly. We walk on the sand at low tide, we paddle, we swim, we love to watch other people at the beach, and to gaze out over the sea towards the windfarms and the horizon. We are comforted by the rhythm of the tide and the sound of the sea. I love the beach but I have a house close to the sea. Why would I need to spend time in a hut? I know that I am missing something as many of my beachside neighbours own or hire huts. There is so much more I need to understand.

Anna on her bench seat in *Pearl*

4 — BUYING

> "The market for beach hut sales is private and largely
> unregulated and its success is dependent upon trust
> and confidence based on past history. Tendring
> District Council beach hut sites are currently only
> offered on the basis of a one year site licence. Despite
> the apparent lack of security of tenure, beach huts can
> change hands for significant sums" (Tendring District
> Council Beach Hut Strategy, 2013).

People's stories about buying a hut provide insight into the
ways of behaving and thinking that underpin the transition
from being a person who likes the beach to becoming a
fully-fledged beach hutter. Buying a hut is an adventure, and
is supported by tales of chance, serendipitous encounters,
inheritance and good fortune. It involves a sort of magic, the

alignment of the stars and fate being on your side. Beach huts are sold privately or through estate agents, however there continues to be a mythology surrounding the process of buying and selling a hut. People tell me that in general the process of purchasing a hut is challenging and that beach huts are in short supply. However, everyone explains that their own experience was straightforward. They see a hut that they like, agree the price with an owner and then buy it. They consider their own ease in buying a hut as an exception.

When I meet Marion and Frank, they are sitting in the sunshine on the promenade. They have had their beach hut on The Leas for 44 years and tell me that when they bought it the Council administered the waiting list, managed all sales and also acted as the arbitrator of what was a fair price:

> "People didn't sell them privately and the process of buying and selling huts was run by the Council. In those days you were on a waiting list and if you refused two, you went to the bottom of the list. We were offered one in the second row but we wanted one on the front and so we turned it down. Luckily a couple of weeks later we were offered this one. In those days if you and the seller couldn't agree a price they would intervene and set a price. Our hut was on sale for £250 but I knocked the price down and we paid £240".

Dierdre has had a beach hut on High Wall since 1966:

> "You had to wait two years for a site then, had to go on

the waiting list and only Frinton people could have them. That is when they were reasonable. I paid £50 for mine and my husband had to wheel it down from near The Walings, right along to our site here. And then when they opened it up to everyone and got rid of the list, the prices went sky high".

The people who tell me the most detailed stories about the process of buying a hut tend to have moved within the last decade. When I meet Karen, she is sitting inside her hut waiting for the kettle to boil. Her husband and two good friends chat just outside on the promenade. Karen tells me that they regularly visit the hut with these friends and that they have all known one another for years. None of them live close by and they are staying on a touring caravan site a few miles away. Karen is a retired nurse and has memories of visits to Walton when she was a child. She has always wanted to own a beach hut and spent her working life dreaming that she would buy one. As she dreamed, she collected mugs, cushions, signs, and postcards for the beach hut she would own one day. There is an element of serendipity in her story about buying her hut:

"I always had this secret ambition that one day if I could afford it, that I would have my own beach hut. When my mother died and she left me a little bit of money and I thought I am going to buy a beach hut now. We arranged to meet the agent to see a couple of huts, but got here a bit early and my brother saw this one had a

'for sale' sign on the door. We thought 'that's a nice
position because it is right by the slope. No steps to get
down to the sea , and also being high up you have a
birds-eye view when the children are on the beach'. My
brother said 'that would be lovely I am going to phone
up'. The man on the other end said 'it's not my hut... the
owner lives in Jersey and he's asked me to sell it for him.
Yes, I can come down right now and show you inside'.
So, he came down, opened it up and there was nothing
in here at all except one of these seat boxes — right here.
And it wasn't boarded inside and it was just creosote
colour and we thought 'ooooh that's perfect'. And it was
a bargain price as the gentleman wanted just to get rid
of it and he didn't need a lot of money for it. So, it didn't
cost us a lot of money! It was a bargain compared to
what the market value was. So we snapped it up".

Debbie has had a hut in the front row at Southcliff for nine
years and she visits two to three times a week in the summer
and a bit less in the winter. When we meet, she is sitting on
the promenade with her sister-in-law. She tells me that she
lives locally and it takes about 30 minutes to walk along the
beach from her home to the hut. Chance also played a part
Debbie's decision to buy her hut. One morning, shortly after
she moved to Frinton she noticed a hand-written card
advertising a hut for sale in the local newsagent window.
She was just settling into her new home and was not looking
for a hut. She tells me that she is not normally impulsive but

the idea of having a hut captured her imagination and she
immediately rang the number:

> "The lady must have just put the card up because I
> phoned her before she got home. And her husband
> didn't even know that she had put it up for sale. But he
> was OK about it as they were going to move!
>
> At first, my husband didn't want a beach hut. He
> said 'What do you want a beach hut for? We live right
> on top of the beach'. It was February when we went to
> look at it and he was complaining all the way that it
> was such a long walk. I kept on reminding him 'but it
> is a nice walk'. He was anti the idea of a hut until we
> got here and looked inside. He immediately said 'I love
> it' and I said 'So do I' and so we bought it".

There is an element of surprise around some purchases.
Anna tells me:

> "We had been talking about getting a beach hut for a few
> years and we had looked at a few. And then at
> Christmas unbeknown to me, my husband looked at
> *Pearl* and he organised the purchase. So on Christmas
> morning we opened a little gift bag with some keys in it.

Carol says:

> "We moved to Frinton in 1984 and one day shortly after
> we moved, my husband went out for a walk in the
> morning with our dog. A bit later he said 'Shall we go

for a walk along the prom' and then while we were walking he said 'Would you like a beach hut?' And I said 'Yes, I would love one' and he said 'How about that one?' He had already bought it that morning. So, thank goodness I didn't say no".

Lynette's first two huts were located on Southcliff and she currently has three beach huts on Eastcliff. She tells me about buying her first two huts:

"I didn't know much about beach huts but my daughter had some money left by an uncle. She wanted to buy something which was in his memory and bought a beach hut in Walton-on-the-Naze. I was living about 10 miles away at the time and when I came to visit, I couldn't believe it. The beach hut was on the front row and once you were inside it felt like you were in another world. I thought 'I would like one of these', so I started to enquire and within a few of weeks I bought a beautiful old hut. It had belonged to a family for generations... I loved that hut. Then about three years later I decided to have a walk up the cliff. I got up onto C and D rows where the view is fabulous. There was a hut for sale and so I bought it. Yes, I was the king of the castle there!"

As Lynette talks it becomes apparent that each hut is heart purchase, each bought spontaneously on the basis of gut-feelings about a particular place or hut.

I have tea with Steph in the hut that she regularly visits which is owned by her mother-in-law. She explains that her parents and their close friends bought beach huts adjacent to one other when she was a child:

> "Both sets of parents bought the huts when we were four. It was extremely lucky that the huts came up next to each other and both my parents and their friends could afford them. They cost about £150. We got the huts, did them up and then both families spent our summers here".

In 2021, I meet two couples who have only just bought their huts and were in the process of settling in. Paul and Vicky are retired and found their hut on The Leas via an agent and are spending their second day at the hut. Vicky tells me:

> "We live over an hour away in Suffolk which meant we couldn't come down that often to search for a hut. In the past whenever we used to come to Frinton we would see the 'hut for sale' notices, but at the beginning of 2021 they didn't seem to do that so often. So, when we wanted to buy one it was a question of going on-line to see when one would come onto the market along this stretch of the beach. Eventually, we came along to view two last Friday. We saw this one on The Leas, and another one along High Wall. We preferred this for the position and then we negotiated the price down until it was OK. Because at the moment they are over inflated in price".

Two days later, by coincidence I meet Lindsey and Robert, who have just bought the hut that Paul and Vicky had viewed on High Wall. Robert tells me that they bought it from an agent and that the process was relatively straightforward. He contrasts this with their attempt to buy a flat in Frinton which is proving to be drawn out and complex:

> "We live an hour away and are in the process of buying a flat in Frinton. It will initially be a second home but we think that we might move here when we retire. We thought we will see what it is like and maybe we will stay here. It is a toe in the water job really. I have no experience of beach huts at all but wanted one because we can retreat here when we come down to the sea. It is somewhere to disappear to in the heat of the day and a place to come when everyone has gone and then you have got the beach to yourself".

In October, I bump into them at their hut again. It is early evening and Robert is warming up after a cold-water swim. They finally completed on their flat at the end of September after repeated delays throughout the summer and contrast the complexities of flat buying with the simplicity of buying a hut. Despite the ease of buying their hut they still have a sense of serendipity in finding a hut in the perfect place.

These stories illustrate a range of experiences. Some people find their huts through estate agents, or on websites but more often they are bought and sold through a more

informal process. Many purchases are impulsive and
happen when people see notices posted onto the front of
the hut, or in the local newsagent's window, or hear about
a hut through friends. At one level buying a hut is relatively
straightforward and mundane as long as you can cope with
insecurity of tenure, are not too fixed on your location
preference, and have the money. The magic happens as the
tale is told and retold and becomes layered with
pleasurable experiences. The chain of events involved in
buying a hut becomes one of the many beach hut tales. A
story to be recollected and shared with friends, a story
about a place that is 'just perfect' and a decision that 'was
meant to be!'

POSSESSING

Some families have owned their beach hut for decades and
tell me that ownership is passed down through the
generations. However, most explain that they have not
owned the same hut for the entire period. There are many
reasons people buy new huts. I hear about family huts being
swept away by the North Sea floods in 1953 or in the more
recent tidal surges in 2013 and 2017. Some moved to
different locations when the huts on Southcliff were cleared
for a couple of years in the 1960s while the Council
undertook work to the promenade. I meet some people
who completely replace their huts about once a decade.
Others choose to repair their huts and tell me they have
undertaken so many repairs over time that very little of the

original structure still exists. I speak to people who decide to move to another hut when they get older, or have young children and need easier access from the road.

Long-time hut ownership is common but visitation fluctuates at different life stages. People talk about visiting most frequently during their own childhood, when they have young children, and again when they have grandchildren or when they retire. Most say that they visited less in their teenage years and in their 20s. They give many reasons for this but the most common are that they wanted to be independent, to do more exciting things, to visit different places, or that this was a time when they were very focussed on working and studying.

Most beach huts are shared, and whilst they might be formally owned by one particular member of a family, they are usually made available to multiple generations and across friendship groups. Sometimes shared ownership is formalised, with several people having joint responsibility for the hut and site fees being shared. More often the hut officially belongs to one person but the key (or key code) is widely available to family and friends. Karen says:

> "I've given my brothers keys so that if they are ever passing, and are in the mood, they can let themselves in. And they have brought their grandchildren, when it is their birthday, for a party or a day at the seaside".

Margaret's family live locally and all use her hut:

"I used to rent one along this row when my children were little for the six weeks of the summer holidays each year. I am retired now and we decided to buy this about seven years ago. Three generations of my family live in Frinton and the hut is regularly used by the whole family. Both of my daughters have keys and are free to use it when they want. We all visit at different times, sometimes together and other times alone".

Dorothy has had a beach hut for 35 years and when we meet she is sitting outside her hut with her husband, while her daughter and grandchildren play on the beach. She lives in Colchester and does not come very often as her husband likes to be active and would rather sail than spend a day just relaxing at the hut. Her children have moved away from the area and so the grandchildren do not visit often:

"I own it with five other families. When my children were small it was convenient. We all had very young children and we could keep potties and changing mats and nappies down here, and not have to carry them backwards and forwards. We used to come a lot when the children were small. It was really great because they could all be here together. It really was a wonderful thing in those days. And now we have all started using it again because we have got grandchildren and it is coming into its own all over again".

Helen's parents bought a hut in the 1990s:

> "because the grandchildren had started coming along
> and Dad's parents were still around. And so they
> wanted a place where four generations could spend
> time together. They wanted to spend weekends just
> sitting by the beach with the grandchildren".

Both grandparents and parents are no longer alive and the
four sisters share ownership:

> "At the moment we don't get down very often, but what
> we do now is that we let friends use it. Just people we
> know. A friend of mine from work was down with her
> two children and her mother yesterday. She has come
> down about six times this summer. She loves it and loves
> bringing her mum. So, we let friends use it and lots of
> them come with their families".

BEACH HUT PRICES

Over the past decade there has been an increased interest in
small buildings. There are an abundance of books extolling
the virtues of cabins, shacks, bothies, treehouses, garden
rooms and sheds (including *Cabin Porn*, *A Women's Shed*,
Tiny House). Some focus on aesthetics and are supported by
images of picture-perfect shacks in isolated locations with
beautiful interiors and well-designed, innovative solutions
to the challenges of constrained space and being off-grid.
Others explore the experiences of being close to nature,

often harking back to a time when life was less complicated. Small buildings enable people to explore the pleasures of getting back to basics, enabling them to retreat from the pressures of modern life, to slow down and switch off.

Our interest in these small structures has been heightened by televisions programmes such as George Clarke's *Amazing Spaces* which celebrates the pleasures of designing innovative small spaces. In 2021, contestants in Alan Carr's *Interior Design Masters* are challenged to create stylised and attractive spaces within some of the beach huts on Southcliff in Walton. Huts have become more desirable, not just because they provide a base, and a few home comforts at the beach, but because many now have quirky or shabby-chic designs which can easily be incorporated into people's social media stories-of-self. Social media posts have contributed to the shift away from the 'friendly pensioners' image of hut dwellers in Tom Boltons book *Low Country* and towards an activity that is bang-on-trend. The beach hut now provides the backdrop to a stylish life, the luxury of simplicity, and is no longer seen as a relic from the past or the preserve of pensioners. This is apparent when in 2020 Sophie Hinchcliff or 'Mrs Hinch', an influencer with over 4 million followers on Instagram posts images of a day at the hut at Eastcliff in Walton.

Our renewed interest in small simple spaces is boosted further in 2020 and 2021 when the challenges and restrictions associated with Coronavirus mean that people spend their holidays close to home. It is unsurprising in this context that the demand for beach huts and their prices soar all around the UK. Hut prices in Walton and Frinton rise quickly but are much cheaper than those in most South coast resorts. While they are not rural, isolated or suitable for overnight use (and therefore unlike the idyllic huts in many books) the huts at Walton and Frinton do provide a relatively affordable space from which to access a beautiful sandy beach with views over the sea. What's more, these huts are close to London and accessible for regular day-trips.

Media interest fuels speculation and in my conversations in 2021, stories about beach hut values proliferate. Beach hut owners share tales of huts going for £50,000, then £60,000 and as the season progresses climbing to over £70,000. These tales are supported by media stories and details of several beach huts in Frinton prominently displayed in estate agent windows. Many owners decide it is time to cash-in, and an abundance of huts come onto the market. Some are sold through agents, some through specialist sites and others more informally through Facebook, signs on doors, and word of mouth.

The boundaries between reality and myth about these price rises are blurred. In May 2021 the BBC runs a story about a women who had bought a beach hut in Walton-on-the-Naze for £10,000 and then had it revalued for £40,000 in 2021. The Guardian reports that the same women bought a hut for £10,500, refurbished it and then sold it for £48,000.

Many of the existing owners are shocked by the current prices and wonder why people would be willing to pay so much. In 2022 Carol says:

> "There is one for sale just down by where my old hut was... It is £60,000. It is £60,000 and it's only a shed".

Her beach hut neighbour Deirdre agrees and asks why anyone would spend so much money on buying a wooden shed. She wonders if the people buying huts now assume that they are also buying the land.

While it is clear that values have risen, it is difficult to verify the actual prices that people pay for their huts. The people I meet who have just bought huts in the most desirable locations tell me that they negotiated and paid considerably less than the list price. Even with the price rises, it is hard to see the huts as a 'sure-thing' investment. On 12 September 2021, I look on two listing sites (www. beachhuts4hire.co.uk and www.rightmove.co.uk) and find 30 huts for sale in Walton and Frinton with prices ranging from £19,000 in the back row at Southcliff to £85,000 on The Walings. Half of the huts available at this time are listed at prices under £40,000 and many had been on the market for the entire summer. On 21 September 2022, I look at the two listing sites again. This time I find 46 huts for sale priced between 20,000 in Walton and £80,000 on The Walings. Half have been on the market since the start of the school summer holidays and three have been on the market since 2021. Clearly not everyone has been able to cash-in on the boom. On walks along the promenade, I identify many more huts for sale informally through notices pinned to front doors. Huts can be purchased all along the beach — the most expensive are on the Walings and the cheapest on the upper slopes at Southcliff. A large number of huts are on the market. Supply appears to exceed demand, and prices have settled.

Paul and Vicky bought their hut in May 2021 and they realise that the price they paid was high. Paul says:

> "I don't think the price will go up much further but I think the prices will stay up while so many people are taking staycations. However, I don't think these inflated prices will hold because people will go abroad when they can. We bought this hut for the long-haul and hopefully when my son and daughter inherit it, they will still get the money back".

As I draw this chapter to a close, I wonder whether inflated beach hut prices will change the nature of a beach hut person, perhaps pricing many local people out of the market. Most of the new hut owners I meet are not from the immediate locality, but none live far away, Vicky and Paul are from Suffolk, Robert and Lindsey are from Brentwood, Nina is from Bishops Stortford, and Anna and Glenn are from a village just outside Kelvedon.

I first met Sarah in *The Waves* in 2019 and since then she has sold her hut:

"There was a big demand for beach huts during 2021 and the prices rocketed to ridiculous prices. I lost a lot of my work during the Pandemic as I do after school tutoring and invigilating and both these areas are zero hours work and I was not entitled to any support. Anyway, we made the difficult decision to sell our beloved hut and we were able to pay a big chunk off our mortgage.

We sold to a family who have been renting a beach hut along our row for many years and had always loved *The Waves*. They were very happy when our beach hut came up for sale and immediately bought it. We are very happy that *The Waves* continues to be enjoyed by such a lovely family".

Emma also sells her beach hut *Costa da Lotta* in 2021 to a rental business, 'Walton on the Naze Beach Huts'. She has some regrets about selling, but was offered a lot of money for it. She co-owned the hut with her brother and it was too expensive to buy him out. She lives locally and intends to continue renting a hut on Eastcliff each year:

"It makes sense to sell and on the plus side, we won't have to pay the site fees, insurance, maintenance. Also my children are teenagers now and so we visit the hut less often".

It is difficult to tell how the price rises will affect the demographic of the beach hut community and the experience of being a beach hutter. I wonder if locals might be priced out of the market but as I collect stories for this book, I discover that many choose to hire as they do not want the responsibility and costs associated with owning a hut. The emerging beach hut strategy appears to allow more opportunities for rentals. At the time of writing, it seems that all hut owners will be able to rent their huts for up to ten days and licences will be issued for those businesses who let out multiple huts on a commercial basis. So, despite the price rises it seems that local people will still be able to engage in some of the pleasures of being a beach hutter as the rental market expands.

5 — STYLE

Beach hut aesthetic is varied and people adopt widely
different approaches to maintaining, decorating and
furnishing their hut. Some are influenced by contemporary
trends in beach hut design with colour coordinated pastel
exteriors and interiors, bunting, pretty Victorian crockery
and fashionably mismatched tables and chairs. Many are
seaside themed, their walls, cushions, crockery and tea-
towels adorned with images of beach huts, starfish, seagulls,
fish, and boats. The approach to interior design is light-
hearted and sometimes ironic. Some huts incorporate
nostalgic imaginings of the past. For example I see several
with 1950s styling incorporating old kitchen units and
formica tables and others displaying collections of
ornaments and prints from the 1960s and 1970s. Some huts
are themed around an idea or a colour. *Sandy Feet* has been

themed as a Tiki bar with its interior lined with bamboo. *Ladybird* is full of ladybird designs and books. *Micky* and *Minnie* are themed around the Disney's cartoon mice.

Designing and decorating is a pleasurable pastime for many beach hut owners, providing opportunities to be playful, to test DIY skills and experiment with layouts and ideas. Innovation is important and people experiment with multi-functional furnishings and fittings. They adapt these small sheds into comfortable retreats, with cooking facilities, storage and changing areas and indoor seating.

While detailed designs differ, people's approach to styling a hut falls into one of three broad types.

1. Designers: Start from scratch, creating their beach hut style is a central pleasure in having a hut.
2. Embellishers: Add to what is already there and develop a theme as they become familiar with the hut.
3. Utilitarian/No Frills: Have little interest in the design of their hut.

DESIGNERS

For the designers, restyling a hut is one of its core pleasures. They develop a clear theme for the design of their hut and research different types of paints and colour palates before starting any major work. They often look at lifestyle sites such as Pinterest for ideas, and engage with other hut owners on Instagram as they refurbish their huts. They usually do the majority of the work themselves.

Jemima buys her hut *Puddleduck Palace* in 2020, and immediately starts to redesign it:

> "It was dark grey when we bought it. The front was rotten and there was nothing inside except a bench. It was a project that hadn't been finished. We did loads of research whether you should stain it or paint it and then into what sort of paint was best for beach huts. I chose the colour — so the outside is Farrow and Ball — Nancy's Blushes — my grandma was called Nancy and inside is Middleton — after Kate Middleton. The hut is my place... it is quite pink, quite girly, quite mine!"

I ask whether her approach to designing the hut is different from designing her home. She laughs and says:

> "I would never have light pink in my house. So, nothing like this. I went pastel because with a beach hut you can. It's a childhood thing, a thing about Wendy houses, about having something which is not what you would have at home. There used to be colour restrictions but now you can have what you want and they are painted all different colours — a mishmash of reds pinks, greens, blues, whites. Pastels are very pretty, with a bit of Cath Kidson thrown in for good measure. I wouldn't dare have a house like that... EVER! It is not my cup of tea at all. It is like an alter-ego. You can have it however you want it".

While some aspects of her hut design are whimsical and playful, others are practical and the layout of its small interior supports a range of different work and leisure activities:

> "A lot of beach hut people just chuck stuff in and then come and sit out on the deck. They use it as a sandy storage shed. My beach hut is not sandy! There is a gap at the end of the worktop there so that I can stack all the chairs behind the gingham curtain. It is neat and tidy and a useable space all the time because I like to work down here. I changed mobile phone network so I could get a signal here. I tether my laptop and I can work here all day. I love working with the sound of the sea in the background. It is just perfect — peace and quiet away from home. I plan to come here over the winter, and I have bought a little heater and I have a perspex sheet for the window to keep out the wind".

Nina set up a beach hut rental business (www.ladybirdseascapes.com) and has taken a design-led approach to renovating and styling her beach huts. She bought her first hut *Ladybird* in 2019 and painted it red and white. Its interior has been carefully curated to include:

> "An eclectic mix of kitsch and vintage pieces with a modern twist and plenty of Ladybird elements... from glass painted Ladybirds to gifted painted pebbles, a

super funky vintage Ladybird kettle and a small
collection of quirky Ladybird Books".

She bought her second hut in 2020:

"I was going to call it Jitterbug and theme it as an
American Diner. I bought some stuff on that theme...
probably enough to kit out about 5 different beach
huts. Then the Alan Carr *Interior Design Masters*
programme set a beach hut challenge at Walton and
someone did an American Diner theme at a hut called
Harley. I didn't want the same as someone else and so,
I completely scrapped the idea.

Then we went into lockdown and so we couldn't
visit. I started to look around for other ideas and saw
Sam's picture on Instagram (www.samuelthomasart.
co.uk). I loved it and messaged him. And he said 'by
the way if you know anyone who has a beach hut that
needs transforming... it is something I have always
fancied doing'. I thought about it and I was so excited.
We first talked at the end of January 2021 at a time
when we were not allowed to meet. Sam came up very
quickly with the design which is the view from here
and is adapted from one of my photos.

We didn't meet until the April when the country
reopened after lockdown and he came to paint the
mural. It felt like a statement and symbolic of sharing
the happiness and joy that we were feeling. We added
the freedom bit at the end because we felt free. People

were out and about again — going for seaside walks. And being here and doing this it was all positive, positive, positive. It felt like it was about time we all start living again".

Since then Nina has bought a third hut, *Dragonfly* which is styled with a secret garden theme.

Anna and Glenn are refurbishing *Pearl*, and share images of the refurbishment on Instagram, posting their first image on the 31st December along with commentary:

> "Our first visit to our new hut, in my happy place, Frinton. The hut has been well looked after structurally but she needs some love and 'beautifying'. Our first job is to try to stop the rain getting in the front door and hatch. Then the plan is to remove the internal doors, kitchen top and bench seat so that we can clad the walls. We will then install a kitchen along the back wall, add new flooring and build a new bench seat (big enough to lounge on and take in the beautiful view). We will have to redesign/replace the door/shutter at the front and of course paint *Pearl* a pretty colour. No doubt we will have some hiccups along the way but this is the start of our beach hut renovation".

They continue to share images and commentary throughout 2022, and by the beginning of October have shared 85 posts. They share insights into their decision-making processes about the type of paint and colours that they will use and regularly post images of the work-in-progress. I meet Anna during the summer of 2022 to talk more about the design of her hut:

> "When we came there was a partition and a lot of bare wood. We wanted to brighten it up, paint it, and make it light. We felt that it would be better if we opened it up. My husband Glenn is a designer and he is very much... 'you need to look at the colour palate — look at what colour goes'. So, before we started the work, we looked at the colour palette and I knew that I wanted the pinks, purples and blues. And then I did a lot of research on Instagram and Pinterest. There is a beach hut company on Mersea and they had done up their huts quite nicely and I had seen their set up. We knew we needed a box for storage for all of the beach toys, the chairs and everything. We wanted to make that space something you could sit on as well.
>
> Our friend is a carpenter and he came and helped. He cladded the walls and put the bench seat here. I wanted to be able to sit here in the corner and look out and see everyone go past and see everyone as they are playing. We saw pictures of another beach hut in Walton with an IKEA kitchen and it looked great and so my husband and friend put one in. We thought that we would have bare wood floors but the boards were not too good and so we just got something we could sweep out easily".

Unlike Jemima their approach to designing their hut reflects their taste in their house where they also opt for bright colours and contemporary design.

Anna introduces me to her beach hut neighbour Roger. He is a kitchen designer, lives locally and has owned a hut for less than two months. His design background is apparent as he starts to explain the possibilities associated with refurbishing the hut. The walls have been clad and lights inserted into the ceiling which are powered by a car battery. He is spending his time researching colours and collecting fabrics swatches in his attempt to recreate a mid-century tea room. The design of the interior of his hut is nostalgic, influenced by his childhood memories of beach holidays in Bogner:

> "My memories of a rented hut were sticks of rock and ice creams. It is those memories which have led to my ideas about what I want to put in the beach hut. I remember going to tea rooms with my gran and with my mum and I just thought I want to harken back to that time and create a 1950s tea-room. I am looking for 1950s linoleum and have chosen this 'granny's pinny' fabric for the cushions and curtains. I am painting the inside neutral with school or NHS green".

He shows me a set of silver-plate fish knives and forks with bone handles and tell me that they were left to him by his parents and that they are ceremoniously brought out for fish and chip and champagne suppers at the hut. He is planning to buy old tea-room posters, an old-tea set and a three-tier plate for cream teas.

EMBELLISHERS

Interior design is not a major concern for some beach hut owners. Embellishers maintain their huts and often paint them pastel colours, but tend not to change the interior configuration. They start their beach hut collections in an ad-hoc manner and generally opt for a beach theme, or vintage or floral design.

Catherine and George have had their beach hut for six years and have made few changes to its interior. They visit at least once a week and spend time at the hut all year round. The previous owner warned them not to make it too smart to avoid being targeted by vandals:

> "He had it for 17 years and he said he used the cheapest fence stain he could get and that he would stain it every couple of years. We painted it four years ago and we have just painted it the same colour again".

They have not changed its configuration and it has a traditional design with interior doors to provide some privacy. They are not particularly interested in redesigning their hut, but decided to repaint the interior to brighten it:

> "It was very dark and dingy because the previous owners had a dark ceiling. We did not change much. Just a lick of paint and brightened it really".

When they first moved they thought the hut would just be a base for beach visits and a place to store beach toys. George built a narrow veranda to create a place to sit just outside the hut. Catherine was not interested in the interior design initially but tells me that family members started to make things for their hut. Her son's girlfriend made a cushion cover for the bench seat and some matching bunting. Friends often arrive with gifts for the hut and its interior has become very colourful, a mix of yellows, blues and greens. She now spends more time embellishing the interior and likes the element of fantasy and the sense that she can do anything.

When Linda and Nick bought their hut it was a brown shed with basic fittings and a curtain to provide privacy for changing. They have refitted the kitchen and added some new cushions to the storage/seating box at the back. Choosing decorations for the hut is an ongoing process. They often pick up things in second-hand shops and have chosen a seaside theme. There are two lifebuoys on the walls which were found on a holiday in France, a display of ornamental fish on the rear wall, and two metal octopuses near the apex of the roof at the front and rear of the hut. They couldn't decide what colour to paint it and laugh as they tell me that they have had many opportunities to experiment. They are on the promenade and have to paint it regularly due to the storms, sun and constant sea-spray. They experiment with a new colour each time they paint and it has been green, yellow and blue. For Nick painting provides an opportunity to switch off and is part of the pleasure of having a hut.

Debbie was not initially interested in the design of her hut:

> "We bought it from an elderly couple and it was brown and dark inside, so we whitewashed it. We give it a coat of paint every now and then — inside and outside and it has been a few colours.
>
> When we first moved here, we changed the kitchen a bit and put in a white worktop. Since then, we have just made it beachy and have put up some bunting. People bring us so much beach themed stuff. Now the hut is full and I have a whole beach themed room at home. At some point, we are going to replace the hut completely, or totally refurbish it, and I already have a lot of things for the new hut".

Dawn and Tina are from Colchester and regularly visit their parents' beach hut with their children. Her parents were not interested in decorating the interior of the hut and so the sisters took charge. They wanted to create an interior which would work for all the generations and was quaint and nostalgic and have not collected any beach themed artifacts:

> "We went a bit twee... a bit 'Cath Kidson' type of thing. I suppose we are trying to make it like a little cottage. We gutted it and decorated it and everything is very pretty. Me and my sister basically came up with the theme and I made the bunting".

Cath Kidson's name crops up regularly in beach hut stories and her designs appear to encapsulate a particular kind of Britishness that people want to express as they decorate their huts. When I check her website in October 2022 her designs include 'Peter Rabbit', 'Queen of Queens', 'Great British Bake Off' and florals such as 'Paper Pansy'. These designs are marketed to women and her website says "Created by women, for women, our beautiful, confident and unique storytelling prints are hand painted with artistry, heritage and heart". Her designs are sold as being "inspired by the creativity, optimism and positivity of those who live life to the fullest".

I think more about the stories that people tell through the design of their beach huts. All the huts I visit provide facilities to support a day at the beach but the stories they tell take us beyond simple pleasures of the seaside and into a fantasy world far away from the worries of everyday life. Beach huts display a 'Wendy-house' domesticity, their diminutive interiors are whimsical, playful and often packed-full with carefully curated clutter.

UTILITARIANS

The third approach to design is utilitarian. The utilitarians regularly maintain their huts but are not interested in designing or embellishing them. These huts providing basic cooking facilities and storage space for beach chairs, toys and equipment. Helen and Anne describe their approach to decorating their hut:

"We come to paint it every year. When we first started you had to do them in the brown stain. They wouldn't let you do colours. Now they are asking everyone to do colours to get away from the stain. Dad used to always paint it 'red cedar' and so we are doing it in 'red cedar'" (Helen).

"We have to do it in 'red cedar' really in honour of dad" (Anne).

"It is very similar to how it was when mum and dad brought it. It is old fashioned, traditional — it is just really simple. We have not gone for trendy because it is not that sort of beach hut really. We have not changed the interior much at all. That bench was there. We put a new kitchen unit in it" (Helen).

"It was brown and we put in a browner one. And we put a new floor down... but we have still got their old beer crate to open the door" (Anne).

"The hooks are all the same. We say one of these days we are going to move those hooks and put some proper ones up but we still haven't done it. We haven't really changed anything. We keep it very simple" (Helen).

Graham's hut is clean and functional. It has some bunting but has not been designed around an overall theme and is a resting place for things his wife does not want at home:

"We just have table and chairs, tennis racquet and

beach balls and crabbing kits. We are going for the rustic look. My wife would go for Neopolitan colours but for me it is more of a camping exercise".

Graham's daughter tells me:

"We tend to bring stuff here that my mum doesn't want in the garden. She bought some bunting with seagulls on but then realised that half of the seagulls are upside down! They were not right for the garden — so they have ended up here".

The idea of maintaining a traditional approach to decorating and laying out a beach hut is prevalent in conversations with people who have experienced beach huts since their childhood. Sue says:

"I just decorated it the way my parents did. All those years ago. So, I've got a storage bench down one side and the cooker on the other. You don't really need anything else because in the end it's a shed".

The design of Steph and Will's huts during their childhood reflected their family interests and beach activities:

"In my hut there were double doors to the changing area — further inside was a cooking area. And my dad was a fisherman — there was the lobster net and fishing stuff in the roof. It wasn't themed... it was more of a functional hut. And Will's family had surfers and windsurfers in the roof... his dad was a keen windsurfer".

Steph has access to her mother-in-law's hut. It is decorated now but she has little interest in the interior decoration:

> "Will and I painted the inside because that is what my mother-in-law wanted. She put the stuff in and chose the orange because it is her hut. My kids have not made anything... it is not their thing. they are more the running around type".

These functional huts normally have a small basic kitchenette, a storage bench, a collection of old folding chairs and deckchairs, a table and a wide array of beach toys. Phillip tells me that these are all that is needed for a good day at the beach:

> "Beach huts should be rough and ready — they are for mucking around on the beach".

When I first meet Lauren, she is sitting outside her family's beach hut with her sister-in-law and they are chatting as they watch their children play on the sand. They are local and visit regularly with family and friends. Lauren works part-time in the family bakery and tells me that she often just pops down for a couple of hours after school or work. The family hut is well maintained but not embellished with ornaments or collections:

> "We don't need to make stuff because it is full of memories".

Like many other utilitarians, Lauren's main interest in

visiting the hut is in spending some of her free-time by the sea. The hut is just a base and holds no particular interest in itself. It is special because it provides a hub for beach activities and family gatherings.

CONVIVIAL SPACES

Whether show-home or shed, beach hut design encapsulates a broad range of ideas about what it is to own a hut and how best to engage in beach hut life. The stories in this chapter illustrate that for many, one of the pleasures of beach hut ownership is the process of creating a convivial base from which to enjoy a day at the beach with family and friends. A beach hut is a stage-set, full of props for an imagined perfect day. It can host a wide variety of activities; play, relaxation, reading, day-time naps, cooking, eating, changing and entertaining. In the early season there is a sense of hope and of anticipated pleasure of the long sunny days that lie ahead. Owners can be seen, paint-pots in hand, working and reworking the tiny interiors of their huts, painting exteriors bright colours.

Beach huts are celebratory spaces and this is reflected in their quirky design. A growing number have murals on the outside and interiors adorned in bunting and fairy lights and the approach to design is joyful and whimsical, providing space for festivity, pleasure and relaxation.

Breakfast at Tiffany's, The Leas

Knitted seagull, Low Wall

6 — CRAFT

For many, crafting is a part of the practice and experience
of being a beach hutter. I am shown hand-made signs,
mosaics, ceramics, paintings, home-sewn cushions and
curtains, knitted rugs, and upcycled furniture. Some huts
display carefully crafted family archives, including
children's drawings, family photographs, and collections of
shells, stones and shark teeth. Each item on display has its
own story and sparks memories and shared anecdotes.

Lynette is an artist and her three beach huts are stylish,
beautifully decorated using a nostalgic theme. She has a
design approach to her rental huts, one has 1950s styling
and the other 1970s. Her own hut is curated but not themed
in the same way as her rental huts. This is the place where
she engages in her everyday practices of being a beach
hutter which include painting, day-dreaming and just

looking at the sea. She shows me some pretty Victorian plates that were left in *Dalriada,* a hut that she previously owned which currently have pride of place in a renovated dresser. These plates spark memories and she tells me about each one in turn. Lynette has painted murals on the walls and ceiling of the interior of her own hut:

"It just happened really. The day I painted the clouds the sky looked like that (points to the ceiling of her hut). I'd come down for a bit of a dream and I was sitting and having my coffee. I thought 'I fancy painting some clouds'. The painting on the back was another idea. I put a mirror up at the back because you can see the sea and the horizon when you stand up. And I thought maybe I could paint the view of what I can see there, reflected on the back wall. I didn't use artist paints. I just used the paints that were here — the blue and cream. And there were two little boats and I painted them up there. I didn't have artists' equipment. I used a terrible old brush that I had down here to touch up the paintwork".

Lynette's murals are combined with a mixture of upcycled, vintage and handmade items:

"I found the dresser by the side of the road. It was damaged and I got a friend to rehang the drawers and painted it. I put the mouldings on and did the tiles and someone gave me the old enamel sink. I love fabrics and I made the curtains and I got the remnants from Kevin Pearce (local carpet and fabric shop). They used to sell the fabric swatches and I bought some of the same fabric in different colours. I made some cushions and bought some in charity shops. That cushion was given to be by a friend and this picture was 99p from a charity shop. I made the bunting — because I do fabric collage as well as painting. This was made from a pair of children's dungarees. I have also made a mosaic of the hut's number".

I identified Jemima as a designer in the previous chapter. This is because when she bought her hut in 2020, she had a clear idea about colour palate, and set out to create a space where she could relax, work and entertain. She likes to make things at the hut:

"Generally, I don't upcycle. At home I buy new stuff. Here the furnishings are a bit of a mishmash. I have upcycled three chairs which are now chalky blue, two were brown, one was white covered in paint. The bench over there was a brown thing and so I upcycled that and my friend made some bench cushions. I found lots of fabrics and I sat here and I sewed for days. I have got a sewing machine at home but I hand stitched all of the soft furnishings for my hut. It is a bit of a labour of love really and I don't want to rush it. I don't want to take it home and run it through the sewing machine there. I want to sit here and take my time. It is not about the end result. It is about doing it. And I don't think it will ever be completely finished. There will always be a little bit left to do".

Melanie likes to make things for her hut and it is full of handcrafted items including a quilt, two crocheted seagulls and a thick pile of brightly coloured knitted blankets. She stitched curtains and cushion covers using fabric from a local charity shop, and painted a picture of a beach hut which now hangs on the wall. The hut is jam-packed with handicrafts, but she keeps on knitting, and having run out of space has started 'yarnbombing' in Walton. In 2022, she crochets two post box toppers, one of a beach hut and the other a chip eating seagull called Sea-Cil. Yarnbombing is her contribution to the streetscape in Walton and is designed to make people smile. Sea-Cil the crocheted seagull enjoys an eventful summer and becomes a local character with a story of his own which is shared on the local Facebook page. At one point he 'migrates' to an unknown destination. Local people lament his disappearance and then, as if by magic, he returns. The details of his journey remain a mystery. As he settles back onto his post box he is slightly the worse for wear and has a peculiar smell, but is otherwise intact. When I visit Melanie in October, Sea-Cil has been washed and is overwintering in the eaves of her hut. He sits contented, with his bag of knitted chips by his side awaiting his next adventure.

Emma's family have had huts for three generations and she talks about her mum making things for her hut *Costa da Lotta*:

> "We painted the inside white. Mum was very good at DIY so she made a fitted kitchen for it, an oven, a grill, two hobs and all the cupboards. She put a lot of love and sweat and tears into it. And then she made all of the cushion covers. They were blue and white chequered cushions, hand- sewn with 'I do like to be beside the seaside' on the back of them. Then my brothers mother-in-law made a decoupage beach hut sign. Mum took a lot of pride in the way that it looked inside".

Collecting things for the hut is a common pastime and is another aspect of crafting at the hut. Some collections are curated around a design theme, some become mini-galleries for kitschy collections and others are the accumulations of treasures from days on the beach, such as photographs and shells. Beach huts are a place to display old seaside postcards, amusing signs, treasures from local charity shops, a resting place for funny, sentimental and sometimes garish ephemera. Many beach hut owners talk about the pleasure of going to the local charity and junk shops in search of second-hand treasures to adorn the hut.

When she is not knitting and sewing Melanie likes to collect things for her hut. The shelves are full of vintage blue pottery souvenir jugs and cups, fragments of china and her family's collection of souvenir spoons from the places they visited during her childhood. Curating and displaying these materials are a key part of her enjoyment of owning and spending time at her beach hut.

Fred says he was unconvinced when his wife said she wanted a beach hut because he thought it was "the most expensive shed you can buy". In addition to his concerns about the expense he didn't like the idea that this would be a place where they would just sit about all day. He doesn't like to be inactive and when they first bought the hut he used to keep himself busy doing maintenance jobs. However, since then he has learned to relax a bit more and has become a beach hut person. Nowadays he loves just spending time sitting and watching the sea or reading. When he is feeling restless he likes to make and collect things for the hut:

> "I made the sign and inside we have a collection of old postcards. You know those old ones which were right on the limit. Saucy postcards with double meanings and so the kids understood one thing and the adults another. We like to look for those old postcards when we are here and we go into town".

Jenny, Geoff and Amy often pick up ephemera from the beach when they visit and then display it in the hut. Amy tells me:

> "The inside is virtually unchanged. We have just added curtains and soft furnishing and a cupboard. And we

all pick bits up as we go along. We look in the local shops and we go for a beach hut theme. We have got a little nook with some random bits we have found on the beach — a toy soldier and some shells".

Like Lynette, many of the hut owners tell me that they have retained some of the ephemera from the last occupants and incorporated it into their new beach hut décor. They see these items as providing a link to the past, and to the previous occupants and as a base for their own collections. Maureen and Phillip own *The Brown Hut* which is now painted blue. The interior structure is unchanged and some of the furnishings from the previous owner are still there. Phillip has put up shelves for decorations which include a carefully curated display of model beach huts, fairy lights, lanterns, beach hut clocks and comic wax candles depicting plump elderly people in beachwear. Maureen tells me:

"The doors were already there and the lady who had it before started the red and white theme and left the spotty curtains. I like to look in the charity shops and have ended up with so many extra things now. We have fun collecting and with the design. It is a play house".

Anna owns *Pearl*, collects art and artifacts as she is refurbishing her hut. She shares the stories of each gift or purchase on Instagram. When I visit, she shows me the pictures on the wall and tells me the tale behind each.

There is a framed picture, drawn by her daughter at the beach hut which shows the family paddleboarding. An image of a pearl in an oyster was created by an illustrator/colleague from work in exchange for a day at the hut. The picture of a beach hut was a gift from a friend to say thank you for organising her hen-do. Anna likes to be creative in the hut and has decorated her mirror to reflect her beach hut theme by gluing on a selection of shells from the beach and some pearls. She loves to shop for the hut:

> "If I like something I will buy it. I love Frida Kahlo and I found these pots with Frida Kahlo images and the pink kind of matched the hut. These vases were in the colours that I like. So, I just pick things up as I go. Every time I go to a shop and see a cushion I like, I buy it".

Karen's hut is full of collections and beach hut memorabilia amassed over many years. Her collection is less curated than many others as much of it has been gifted by other people:

> "When people used to ask what I would do when I retired, I would say 'I am going to buy a beach hut and I am going to sit in it all day. Every day that I can, I am going to be in the beach hut'. And so, whenever it was my birthday people used to say 'look I have found you a lovely mug with a picture of a beach hut', or 'I have found you a lovely cushion with a picture of the seaside', or 'I have found a sign or a hook'. It became a

standing joke. I have bought the odd thing myself, but most of them are things that people gave me because they knew that I had this obsession about getting a beach hut. And they have memories because I can think 'so-and-so bought me that'. I have made my magic board where I collect postcards of funny old men at the seaside with hankies on their heads, and some of those rude ones and the fat lady ones. Oh, and somebody painted me a lovely box — it's painted inside with lovely flowers in it. And I said that it will be perfect because I can stand my deck chairs in it. And I had a nice seat box made. There is storage in there".

The utilitarians do not collect ornaments but many of them like to make things in their huts. Their crafting processes are more akin to the making and mending 'folk skills' identified by Rachel Hunt (2018) in her essay 'On sawing a loaf: living simply and skilfully in hut and bothy'. The utilitarians enjoy spending time in a modest space next to the beach and develop their skills in simple living by recycling and making-do. Frank and Marion have had their hut for 44 years and over time they have slowly refurbished it often using materials that they had at home. Frank worked as a printer but tells me that he always wanted to be a carpenter and he takes pleasure in making things for the hut. The interior of their hut is functional and reflects their interest in recycling and thrift. At the hut they have a sense of camping out and living a simple life.

Marion is in charge of the interior which includes:

> "a mismatch of things I don't need at home — old pots,
> pans and crockery. The cushions were made from the
> cot mattresses that our boys had and I used old curtains
> to make the cushion covers. I made them myself".

Marion and Frank's hut is basic but not sparse. It contains
storage benches, tables and chairs beach ephemera and
cooking facilities.

BRIMFULL

As I compile the stories for this chapter, I consider my
feelings about beach huts. The huts I visit are always full of
possessions. Some things are practical and support a day on
the beach, others are decorative. My instinctive reaction is
discomfort, too much stuff creates a sense of panic. I have
not seen any huts that are sparse and I like sparse! I am
shown collections, crafts, artwork and memorabilia and
discover that the beach hut is a creative space where people
come to knit, paint or sew, and that this stuff accumulates
over time. Even those people who don't set out to curate and
display collections of memorabilia are thwarted by friends
and relatives who bring beach themed gifts whenever they
visit. Some collections are nostalgic, with people retaining
things left by the previous owner as a way of creating a sense
of history and continuity within their huts.

I reflect on my own crafting and collecting practices and
realise that I am not being totally honest with myself. I am

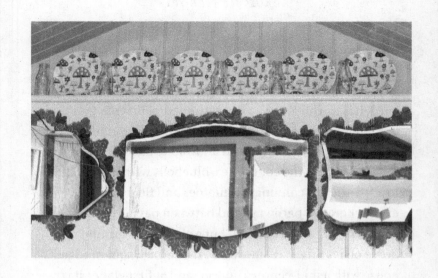

All Of Me Loves All Of You, Southcliff

in denial. O.K. I don't knit or sew, but I garden and I write. These are my crafts, and both are accomplished in the vicinity of my writing 'shed' which sits in the corner of the garden. My house is neat, things have their place, but my garden is unruly, I am an unrestrained plant collector and garden with abandon. Plants pop up in unintended places, and are usually welcome and allowed to stay. There are marigolds with the courgettes, bluebells with the parsley, love-in-the mist amongst tomatoes and fleabane everywhere, on pathways and between paving stones.

I tell myself I don't collect, but a closer look around my home belies this. I live in a white modernist, square edged house with a mid-century interior and at first glance it is sparse. But look closely and you will see the ornamentation. Not everything in this house is a necessity, some items are for display. I have glass. Let's not call it a collection, but on the windowsill is a glass boat, a vase from a friend, and a glass bowl from a trip to Malta. On the sideboard is a glass orb, dimpled, green, an ornament from my grandparents' house. It has no real purpose, but refracts the light, is beautiful and sparks memories of childhood and another house.

And hidden in the drawer, another collection. Notebooks full of words, ideas, notes-to-self. An inspiring phrase from a book, an idea that wakes me in the middle of the night. Jottings for papers never written, notes from writing groups, from my travels. Scribble, scribble, another notebook filled, another notebook filed. Dense forests of words and some illegible rantings. If my writing was

measured by the volume of words jotted in these notebooks
I would be quite something! Then there are the books on
display in my house which tell a story, but behind that story
are the hidden books. The 'too-many' books, secret books
that sit in cupboards, hidden from public view.

The more I look, the more I find. I have an accumulation
of stuff from the beach — those small treasures washed in
by the tide and picked up on walks. Shells, sharks teeth,
sea-glass popped into pockets and then rehomed in my
house or garden.

ENOUGH!

I realise that collecting is an instinctive process for all of us,
but at home I am restrained, my collections sparse,
controlled, and hidden. I realise that I have missed a trick.
For many beach hut people a hut confers a sense of freedom.
It is an alter-ego, a palace of packed-in treasures,
abundance, sensory overload. Interiors are playful, busy
and uninhibited, containing everything you might need
and more. The clutter, crafts and collections simultaneously
tell a story and create a place for pleasant memories to be
stowed to be revisited. I am starting to understand the
attraction of a beach hut and perhaps beginning to develop
a sense of what it is to be a beach hut person.

Tom's Hut, Southcliff

7 — NAMING

I am intrigued by beach hut names and wonder about the
practices associated with naming or renaming a hut. In
April 2019 I walk the 3.7 miles along the beach from the
Walings in Frinton, to Hipkin's beach in Walton noting
down names and photographing hundreds of beach huts.
Job done! I think. But the job is not done. Each time I walk
along the prom I notice that new names have appeared.
In May 2021, I decide it is time for another survey and
discover 112 new names, 92 of which are on huts that were
previously nameless. In October 2022 I survey again and
I find 122 new names, 80 on huts which were not named in
either previous survey. Between 2019 and 2022, 89 huts
have had their name signs removed. Naming, un-naming
and renaming is persistent, reflecting changes in ownership
and a trend towards naming huts.

The most commonly used word in the naming of the beach huts is *Hut,* closely followed by *Beach* and *Sea.* These words are used playfully to denote different things. I type out each name, put them into a table, then read and re-read them looking for patterns or themes. I notice that *Storm Sea* has been renamed *Bliss by the Sea, Mina Mar* has become *Vitamin Sea, Daisy Days* now is also called *Vitamin Sea.* I wonder if there is a trend towards names associated with health and wellbeing. I am intrigued and need to talk to beach hut owners and find out more about naming processes and the meaning of hut names.

1. *Humour and puns*
The naming of huts is often jokey and playful. Some examples include *Peace-a-hut*; *Feeling hut, hut, hut*; *Fruit and hut, Sea-esta, Sea la vie, Seaclusion, Sea for Miles, Seas the moment, Seas the day, Life's a beach, Son of a Beach Hut, Gulls and Buoys, Family Tides* and *Bass Clef (which is located at the base of Southcliff). Coast of Summer* and *Costa Da Lotta* reflect the price of a hut. There are reworkings of the names of TV series — Peaky Blinders becomes *Beachy Blinders,* Starsky and Hutch becomes *Stars, Sky & Hutch.*
Victoria tells me about naming her hut *Windy Bottom*:

> "We moved to Clacton-on-Sea in May 2003 and my favourite place of all was the beach. I had always been envious of beach hut owners and I finally managed to buy one. The estate agent opened the stiff door and as

I walked through, my left foot seemed to sink slowly, taking the lino cover down. I pulled the lino up and discovered a rather large hole, where the floor had rotted away. A surge of wind came through, bringing with it a puff of light sand. I had no worries about this, as I am very fortunate that my husband is a carpenter, so I bought it.

I was excited about my new beach hut and I was telling all my friends about it. I told them I had an affinity with this beach hut, as it also had a windy bottom. My married name is Gusterson and my friends had affectionately referred to me as 'Gusty Bum', so *Windy Bottom* stuck.

I put an order in for a slate *Windy Bottom* sign and I needed to decide whether I wanted plain or countersink screw holes and how many mounting holes I preferred. I emailed the company querying what the strongest option would be, as I didn't want the sign falling off. I couldn't help but laugh... the email response was, 'It's ok, we can assure you your sign won't blow off!'"

Victoria's hut now has a *Windy Bottom* image on the front doors:

"I love the old Victorian postcards with the big cheeky ladies and men and I wanted to incorporate that sort of idea onto the beach hut. I drew a seaside design on two pieces of ply wood, of a man bending down looking through his legs and I painted and varnished it and my husband lined them up and attached them to the door opening. I am one of those people who love to hear the sound of laughter and this has certainly worked for me. Almost everyone that walks past has a little chuckle and it is a good topic for conversation".

2. *Relaxation and positive feelings*

Many names reinforce the idea that the beach hut is a place for relaxation and makes people feel positive. Thirteen huts have names which include the word happy including; *Happy Days (x3), The Happy Hut (x2) Many Happy Returns, Roisin's Happy Hut, Happy Ours, Happy House, This is our Happy Place, Holmans' Happy Hut, Happiness is a day at the Beach Hut, Our Happy Place* and *Happy Place.* Four huts have names which include the word *Joy,* two contain the word *Bliss* and two huts are called *By the sea all worries wash away.*

As the book progresses, more huts incorporate the idea of a hut as a retreat. In 2019, I notice *Jo's Retreat, Theresa's Retreat, Lifes' Retreat* and by 2022, they are joined by *Rose's Retreat, Ava's Retreat, Pete's Retreat, Randy and Juicy's Beach Retreat, Sandy Retreat, Sandy Feet Retreat, Beach Retreat, The Beach Retreat* and *Retreat.* In 2019, there is one hut called *Vitamin Sea* and by 2022, three more huts have adopted this name.

There are now seven hut names which include the word 'rest' including *Forarest, Resthaven, Philly's Rest,*

Windy Bottom, Southcliff

Shannon's Rest, Edith's Rest, Ducks Rest, Cootes Rest, four hut names incorporate the word *Escape* and two huts are called *Seaside Sanctuary*. A hut is an *Oasis, Our Little Bubble,* a place of *Serenity,* that can *Make you right*. It is a place where you spend *Lazy Days (x4)* or *Idle Ours* sitting in *Seaclusion* just *Losing Days*.

3. *A family gathering place*

Family relationships are often evident in the naming of beach hut and include, *Sister's Hut, Nanny's Den, Grandad's Hut, Nanny Edwards, Grannie Annie's, Nana Jo's, Grinny and Pop's, Grandad's Shed,* and *Granma's Wendy House, Family Tides, Daddy's Girls, Nanny Beach* and *Dad's Plaice*. Sometimes beach hut names reflect the surnames of the families that own them such as *The Cook Hut, Hilliers Hut, The Cole Shed, The Brown Hut, The Woods* and *Fisher's Plaice*.

While many family names and relationships are obvious to everyone who walks by some require further explanation. I speak to Susan outside her hut *Bimbo*. I have often wondered about the name — the Oxford Dictionary definition is 'an attractive but unintelligent or frivolous young woman'. It seems an odd name for a hut and I wonder if it harks back to the saucy seaside postcard era. Susan tells me:

> "*Bimbo* is the nickname of my grandfather. As a boy, there were Pierrots (traditional seaside clowns) in one of the shows on the pier. And one of the Pierrots looked

just like grandad apparently, and he was called Bimbo.
So, the local people all named grandad Bimbo. And
right up to the very end my grandmother always called
him Bimmy or Bim. I don't know exactly when the
Pierrots came here, but my grandad was born in 1900.

And sometimes when you are in the hut you hear
people talking about the name *Bimbo* as they walk
along. And they all get it wrong... and you think that it
is not because of that! But I can't change it and my
family wouldn't change it".

Families and friends meet at huts. They are convivial places
which is reflected in some names. For example *The Skaal*
are a tribe of Nords who were known for being welcoming
and hospitable, *Ohana* means welcome in Hawaiian. There
are two huts called *Welcome to the Beach Hut* and one
Whale come to our Beach Hut.

4. *Cultural references*

The naming of many huts reflects popular culture with
references to the names of books, films, TV programmes
and music. The most commonly referenced film is 'Star
Wars' with one *Jabba the Hut, Jabba (x3), Jabbas the Hutt*
and *Sea 3PO*. Other films include *La Dolce Vita, Breakfast
at Tiffany's, Jaws, Sea Biscuit, Paradise Found (x2), Jaws*
and film locations include *Amity Island*.

Four huts are named using catchphrases and characters
from the TV series 'Only Fools and Horses' *Lovely Jubbly,*

Luvly Jubbly, Cushty and *Uncle Albert.* There are two huts called *Yabba Dabba Doo* the catch phrase of 'The Flintstones' and one called *Blistering Barnacles* the swear word used by Captain Haddock. *Micky* and *Minnie* are themed around Disney's famous mice and *Mutley's* after Dick Dasterdly's dog in 'Whacky Races'.

There are a host of huts that are named after characters and places in children's literature, including classics like *The Famous Five* and *The Little Sugar House* by Enid Blyton, *Neverland* the home of J.M. Barrie's 'Peter Pan', *Pooh Corner,* the home of A.A. Milne's 'Winnie the Pooh' and *Twas Brillig* from the 'Jabberwocky' by Lewis Carrol. References to more recent children's books include *Hermoine* from the Harry Potter series, *Gangsta Gran's, Inky Octopus, Dora's Explorers* and *Cedric Seahorse, Seahorse. Puddleduck Palace* refers to Beatrix Potter's Jemima Puddleduck. It is owned by Jemima who tells me that as a child she had all the Beatrix Potter books and ornaments and that people use to make associations between her name and Potter's Jemima Puddle-duck.

I also find huts that are named after songs including *Mr Blue Sky, Bring Me Sunshine, Ob-La-Di Ob-La-Da, I do like to be beside the Seaside, Penny Lane, Happy House* and lyrics *Love Shack Baby, Sail Away With Me* and *Hotter than July.*

5. *Other places*
Many hut names reflect other places such as *Our*

Shangri-la, Xanadu, Bali, Pacific Edge, Atlanta, Sark, Norvic Memories, Pifflex Point. Brooklyn, Clonlea, Taranaki and *Simla*. Lynette is originally from New Zealand and has named her hut *The Bach* which is the word used for the huts there.

When Melanie bought the hut, she retained its name. She tells me:

> "Dalriada is a mythical land between Ireland and Scotland. It has no special connections for me it is just the name of the hut. I know some people change the name of the hut, but I didn't rename it and Lynette (the previous owner) did not rename it. Actually, there is quite a lot of rot at the front in that wood and the sensible thing would be to hack off the name but I am a bit attached to it. You can't even get those kind of letters anymore and this is the way it has always been".

Several huts are named after resorts i.e. *Coco View* and *Pelicans Roost,* and *The Fish Pot* is named as a reminder of a restaurant visited on a holiday in Barbados.

Some signs are in other languages, for example *Il Nostro Posto, Petit Maison en bord de mer, Cwt Traeth Maggie, and Te Whare.* Richard's hut is *E' solo un caponnone* and he tells me about naming the hut:

> "I had an Italian friend and she gave me the Italian for it. I was trying to do it in Latin and so people would ask what it said. 'It's only a shed' is what it is meant to say".

This naming belies its significance in terms of his family relationships and memories that he associates with the hut:

> "I built this because my sister was ill. She had cancer and she and her husband would come to our old hut which was falling apart. So, I built this in my back garden and brought it down".

6. Memories

Marge named her hut *I C the C* and recollects her sense of expectation and excitement when she was a child as the family arrived in their holiday destination:

> "I can remember being in the car with my brothers and sisters, going on holiday and all of us looking for the first glimpse of the sea and then us shouting 'I can see the sea! I can see the sea!"

Debbie tells me about the name of her hut *Beside-La-Cey-Side*:

> "We named it after my dog because when we lived in Hornchurch we had this dog called Lacey. Once we had a dog, we started to have holidays in this country and we bought a touring caravan. We often used to stay in Weeley and we would always come to the beach because our dog absolutely loved it. And really, she was the reason that we moved down here. She has died now and the name is in her memory".

7. *People's names*

Some huts are named after the current owners such as *Lola's Loft, Philly's Rest, Nellie's Nest, Harry's Harbour, Flossie's Den, Jan and Stan's Hideaway, Jasper's View, Archie's Hut, Tom's Hut, Boona's Place. Iris May, Al-Win* and *Chaz's Bequest* remember family members who bequeathed a hut or the money for a hut. *Lil and Phil's* recollect the names of the current owner's parents who regularly visited Walton beach when he was a child.

A growing number of huts have traditional English names which are not the name of the hut owners or a member of their family. Anna tells me about the process of naming her hut *Pearl*:

> We have got Pippa my daughter and Poppy the dog.
> I was lying in bed one night thinking about names
> that relate to the seaside but are still quite catchy. And
> I said to my husband what do you think about *Pearl*
> and he said it sounds like a granny.
>
> I like that because it reminds me of my grandma's
> hut at Mersea which we visited a lot when we were
> children. My grandmother died when I was about 5
> and so my memories of her at the hut are very limited
> but I associate it with her because she did all of the
> sewing for that hut; all of the coverings, all of the
> curtains. So, *Pearl* seemed the right name. And now
> when I say we are going to *Pearl* today people know
> what I mean. We are not just going to the beach we are

going to *Pearl* and it just gives her a bit of character.
I always say her".

Pearl has become an imagined older woman who is very
much a part of the family. Several other huts have adopted
names associated with the older generation... like *Bertha*,
Florence-Grace, and *Maisy*. Sometimes this relates to the
ownership of the hut, and other times a wish to imbue the
huts with a sense of tradition and nostalgia. The biggest
beach hut rental companies often use traditional names for
their huts. 'Walton on the Naze Beach Huts' has *Ellen*, *Nell*,
Lizzie, *Emily*, *Betty*, *Rosina*, *Doll*, *Margaret*, *Winne*, *Mac's*
and *Anne-Marie*. 'Daisy Beach Huts' has *Daisy*, *Rosie*, *Lily*,
Bertie, *Molly*, *Lizzie*, *Poppy* and *Billie* and 'Alice Beach
Huts' has *Alice*, *Florence* and *Lilibet*. These nostalgic
personifications evoke our imagination, reminding us of
childhood seaside rituals and perhaps give us a sense of
spending a day at the hut hosted by a nice old lady.

THE NAMING PROCESS

People tell me about renaming their beach huts. When she
first bought it Karen's hut was called:

> "*Bejam*.... Remember Bejam the Freezer shops which
> are now called 'Iceland'. Well Mr Bejam owned this
> one. I changed the name because I didn't want it to be
> named after a Freezer shop!".

Karen renamed of her hut *The Hutch* reflecting its basic nature and explains:

> "I chose that name years ago... long before I had a hut. As in rabbit hutch... because it is small and cramped".

When I first speak to Lindsay and Robert in 2021, they are just settling in having purchased their hut two days before. They are already starting to think about renaming and redecorating their hut:

> "At the moment it is *Goodevansabove*. So we are planning to do a refurb and rename it. We have some ideas' *Tide waits for no man*', '*Ebb and flow*' but the favourite at the minute is '*Tide and Time*'. We will see which one fits — which one we like".

In October I see them at their hut again. They have a new name:

> "It is called *Ripples and Tipples*- ripples because of the sea and tipples because our neighbours are really friendly here and we are often invited for drinks at the end of the day".

There are a few huts whose name reflects the name of the hut next door. *Mickey* sits next to *Minnie*, *This'l do* is joined by *This'l do 2* in 2022, one of the huts called *Jabba* sits next to *The Hutch*. In Chapter 2, I introduce Sue, Martin and Sarah who I meet in 2019 outside their adjacent huts

Katrina & and *The Waves*. In our conversation Sue explain how the two huts were named:

> "*The Waves* was already named and we thought it would be fun to name the two together. Originally the plan was for a more subtle approach to naming so the intention was *Katrina Anne* but the sign writer misunderstood and added *Katrina &*. He bolted the sign into the shed with two heavy bolts so we had to accept it as it was".

When Sarah and Martin sell their hut in 2021, the new owners change the name of *The Waves* and the sign is removed. For several months *Katrina &* sits on its own — its sense lost without its jointly named neighbour. By the end of the summer the naming conundrum is resolved when the sign from the Waves is moved and the full name *Katrina & the Waves* is resurrected with two signs on one hut. I find out that:

> "*Katrina &* was not a unanimous choice back in the 2000s. There was lots of discussion and it narrowly beat *Surfin'* because the other next-door hut is called *Happy Days. Happy Days, Surfin', The Waves* was not to be. Shame! It would have still worked without *The Waves*".

NOT NAMING A HUT

So far, I have focussed on hut names but many people

choose not to name their huts. So, for example Ruth's family have had huts since the 1950s and she explains that beach huts were named in the 1960s, and then naming went out of fashion:

> "It used to be named but we dropped the name when we replaced this one. It was called *Rosemere*. It was easy just to have the number. A lot of them dropped the names then, but they are being named again now".

Steph's family bought their hut in the 1980s and says:

> "It never occurred to my family to name our hut. It was just a hut. It was 279. Naming wasn't a thing for us".

Margaret tells me that her hut:

> "hasn't got a name, just a number. In Walton, they name them.... They have all got saucy names".

Dorothy points out that naming can be a challenge in huts that are co-owned:

> "Can you imagine five families trying to agree on a name? I think coming up with a name might be the end of a really long friendship".

This challenge is also apparent within some families and Dawn says:

> "We can't decide on a name that we all like so we haven't named her. Everyone else has. I don't know — often

they seem to be a combination of people's names. We thought about naming it after our parents — but mum and dad's names don't really go together".

MAKING SENSE OF BEACH HUT NAMES

For many people the naming of the hut is part of the process of becoming a beach hutter. New hut names often signify the start of an adventure and many names encompass expectations of long sunny days on the beach, relaxing with family and friends. Hut names are light-hearted and playful, and provide the opportunity to express intentions and expectations of the opportunities the hut will provide. Names often signify an emotional attachment to a hut, elevating it, making it significant. A hut is so much more than a wooden shed.

I spend hours surveying huts, poring over names, speaking to people and then I realise that beach hut names tell the story of the beach hut experience.

THE BEACH HUT

I do like to be beside the Seaside,
Happy Days, Bring me Sunshine,
Summer Breeze, Serenity,
By the sea all worries wash away.

Whale come to our Beach Hut,
Seaside Sanctuary, This'l do,
Forarest, Vitamin Sea,
Retreat, Retreat, Retreat.

Son of a Beach Hut, Life is a Beach,
Linger Longer in your Folly by the Sea,
It Costa Da Lotta but it'll Make You Right,
Let's be Frank, This is the Life

Yabba, Dabba Doo, it's Playtime,
Feeling hut, hut, hut?
Going for a Swim,
Skinny Dip, The Cheeky View.

You and me by the Sea,
Breakfast at Tiffany's,
Tea and Toast,
Aloe Vera, Jabba, Jabba, Jabba

The Great Escape,
Paradise Found, Bliss by the Sea,
Making Memories,
Happiness is a day at the Beach Hut.

Ada on the beach, Frinton

NAMING MY IMAGINED BEACH HUT

What would I call my imagined hut? Generally, I don't name inanimate objects. My homes have street numbers not names. My car is not called 'Dave', my writing space is just the shed. I worry that I lack imagination and will myself to dig a little deeper to find a name for my imagined hut.

I ask people for ideas. *The Sea Word* suggests one neighbour as we make our way through a bottle of wine. We laugh boldly, loudly. This is an imagined hut, and there are no consequences. I visualise the expressions of promenade walkers. Some would laugh, but others would tut and wonder what the world was coming to. I imagine the complaints — a letter from the beach hut association or from the Council. I am not brave enough for *The Sea Word* even in my imagined hut.

I search for meanings, associations and am reminded of a photograph of my grandma, aged eighteen, standing alone ankle deep in water on Frinton beach. She is self-conscious in her un-shapely bathing attire. I ask my dad about the photo and discover that she was a lady's maid for Lady Vesey and regularly visited Frinton in the 1920s. The photo does not tell her story, skin deep she is no beauty. But look beyond the surface and you will find the most beautiful person I have ever met. A copy of the photo now sits on display on a side table in my home. The frame is jewelled, ornate and out of keeping with the style of the house, but it befits her status, rendering her divine, and the table an altar. She is my only family connection to Frinton. I name my imaginary beach hut *Ada,* in memory of my grandma.

Swimmers, Southcliff

8 — DAYS

THINGS CARRIED TO A BEACH HUT
A good book
Teabags and milk
Picnic
Towel
Swimsuit
Jumper
Raincoat
A rubber dinghy
Loose change for ice creams
An excited child

SETTING UP CAMP
The tide ebbs and flows, each day revealing freshly washed
sand. As the day progresses this clean damp canvas is

adorned with the temporary constructions and arrangements that support leisure time at the beach. Every day an abundance of stuff is transported down the slopes. Little trailers full of toys and food, inflatable unicorns, paddleboards, kayaks, balls for beach games, kites, buckets and spades. On sunny days, when the tide is out, the sand is covered by a hastily constructed shanty-town, its boundaries delineated by windbreaks, gazebos, open-fronted beach tents, deckchairs, blankets, cool-boxes and sunshades. There is a relentless shifting as day trippers arrive, establish their encampments and then rework them as more people arrive and the tide flows back up the beach. Activity is structured around the tide and weather. Countless sand structures are imagined, crafted, and adorned; sandcastles, forts, villages, mermaids are lovingly constructed. Hours of toil, followed by hasty demolition as they are gleefully jumped upon or inundated by the incoming tide. A day at the beach provides a lesson in impermanence!

For some, a beach hut is predominantly a storeroom for beach paraphernalia, a base from which to unpack and then set up camp on the beach. For others, it is a destination in itself, a place to be close to, but not actually on the beach. A hut provides a vantage point from which to observe people and nature, to be near people but within your own mapped out and bordered territory. Privacy, comfort and a kettle, away from the itchy sand.

ROUTINES

Marion and Frank live several miles outside Frinton and like to visit their hut a couple of times a week throughout the summer. Before they retired, they visited at weekends, but now they prefer to come during the week when it is less crowded. They never visit in the winter, but sometimes come for a few hours in the spring and autumn if the weather is good. Marion describes a typical day at the hut:

> "We unpack, put the kettle on and make a brew. We bring stuff with us and sometimes we have a late breakfast. If we are coming down in the afternoon, we will bring a piece of cake. Today we made some sandwiches down here and we will have something to eat when we get home. We often have bacon sandwiches. Sometimes I sit and read while my family goes swimming. But most of the time I sleep".

As I collect more stories, I discover that for many people a beach hut day is structured around routines involving food and cups of tea. Marge tells me:

> "We always have a cup of tea straight away. We normally bring food down and we might go to the kiosk and get a portion of chips at lunch time".

Terry describes a typical day at the hut:

> If it is just the two of us then we don't do very much. We will probably bring lunch and sit about and read a

little bit. We know quite a lot of people here now, so
we often spend time chatting to people. And we have
friends with a hut at the back on Southcliff so we
know quite a few people there as well. Sometimes we
go for a walk on the beach. We tend to come down
about 12 o'clock. If we don't have visitors then we will
bring our lunch and eat it accompanied by a glass of
wine. We normally like to bring a bottle to the hut".

His wife Olivia adds:

"As people go past, they say 'what a great way to live
— drinking wine and sitting outside the hut in the sun'".

I speak to Phillip and Maureen in 2021 and they tell me
they have a summer routine that encompasses regular
visits to the beach hut. Maureen says in the past they used
to come down early in the morning when nobody was
around and cook a full English breakfast. Now they play
tennis first thing and then come down late morning or at
lunch time. They like to bring food and stay on the beach
late on their own perhaps until 12 or 1 in the morning.
They have put up fairy lights in the hut and particularly
like being there in the dark, just sitting and listening to the
waves. Several times when they have been sitting in their
hut late at night the security guards have knocked on the
door to check that they are not planning to stay overnight.
They tell me that before the Pandemic:

"We used to have barbecues and we would put little

lights out on the beach and we would be dancing".

Sarah talks about her beach hut schedule:

"Well, there is a routine isn't there. When we used to come with my mum we would get here and then think let's have lunch. The food is quite important, and when we visit now we usually have a picnic. If we come with friends everybody brings something to share. And then we have a swim if the tide is in, and we walk. Our big thing is walking along to the toilet! We say who wants to go to the toilet and we walk along together and have a chat and walk back down the beach. We enjoy that going to the toilet sociability".

RELAXATION

For many, the beach hut is a place to relax with a book or newspaper, or just to sit and watch the sea. When people visit their huts alone, they like to read, watch passers-by, and to listen to families playing on the beach and the sounds of the sea. Beach huts provide time away from chores, a place to daydream, to cast adrift or become lost in thought, a place to reconnect with self and with nature. Jemima treasures time there on her own:

"When I am not working and I am here on my own I do nothing. Just nothing. I just sit here and might read a book. When the dog comes down, we go for a walk and then I just shut the bottom half of the door

and he sits in here. So, I have got to have the dog mat
and dog bowl, his 'babies' (toys) and his tin of chews.
It is his place too. He loves it and just sits here quietly".

For Lynette the hut is a place to go to dream. Margaret
brings the paper or a book and just loses herself. Dawn
loves "to sit in the hut and watch the sea".

Anna, Melanie, Carol Dierdre and Margaret explain that
the hut provides an escape from the chores at home.
Melanie likes to:

"read, or crochet, or I might go for a walk. Actually I
don't really do very much! It is a bit weird when you
articulate it... I guess that I am really wasting my time.
I am basically not dealing with stuff at home when I
am here. I am not tidying up, I am not cleaning, I am
not gardening, I am not dealing with things. I think
you either get a beach hut or you don't. I just sit and
look at the view. I used to sail and my favourite bit of
sailing was being moored up with the kettle on and
looking at the sea and looking at the birds. And so this
is like a stationary boat I suppose".

Carol also enjoys the hut as an escape from chores at home:

"A typical day at the hut is for me to bring a book, bring
my lunch and just let the world go by. I am not a
swimmer... I paddle. I come here a lot. It is the only
place where I don't do anything because when I am at
home, I am forever doing jobs".

Deirdre goes to the hut to escape the jobs in the garden:

> "This is my bolt hole. I do not want to sit out in my garden because I see that there is too much to be done so I come down here".

ACTIVITIES

Jemima tells me that a day at the hut depends on who she visits with:

> "When I come with my husband, we are a bit more active. We might not come all day but we will take the dog out for a walk, have a splash around, have a coffee, we will come for dinner and to socialise".

People talk about a variety of physical activities at the beach including kayaking, paddleboarding, beach games and swimming. Amy likes to swim and bodyboard in the sea during the summer months:

> "If it is a really windy, blustery day we will go into the sea. Even if there are really big waves then we will try and go into the sea and we have always done that".

Debbie and her husband like to walk to the hut with the dog:

> "It is just somewhere to go to get out of the house — just somewhere nice to sit and relax. We visit all year around. In winter we often walk here with the dog and then sit outside with our coats on and have a hot drink. When we come down in the summer, we

normally bring breakfast and have a coffee. My husband has got a kayak and he has just bought a paddleboard and so he will go off. I am not into water sports and I potter around in here with the dog. I might read the paper or I sit and watch the people go by. I am quite happy doing that.

When we have friends over, even in the winter we often go for a walk and stop at the beach hut. Sometimes we get fish and chips, sometimes we have a barbecue. We always stop for a coffee. I have got a granddaughter and when my daughter and son-in-law come down, I like to sit up here. I just love to watch them on the beach having fun — the dog playing with bubbles on the beach, my granddaughter playing in the sand or paddling and my son-in-law out on the kayak".

Many people talk about 'people watching' and for Amy the hut functions as a hide:

"We sit on the wall or when the weather is not so good, we just tuck ourselves away in the hut and people watch".

It is a place to retreat and observe people on the beach, to glimpse into other lives and to listen to the beach sounds. Anna has designed her hut so that she can sit on a bench seat with long views along the promenade:

"I love to watch everyone come past. I love to watch

people's happy faces and the kids playing and if people are having barbecues, it is nice to see them together. Everyone is just so happy and friendly here, and it is a different pace of life, and you need that".

RITUALS

When talking about the beach hut activities, many people link their current routines to their childhood memories of being at the hut. Often a day at the beach hut involves a practice of rituals learned in childhood and is a way of enacting long held family traditions. Sue's recollections of her days at the beach hut during childhood merge with a story about her regular activities when she visits now:

"When I was a kid, we would drive from London. My mum would get a big breakfast on and my dad would swim out to the raft. Mum would wave to him when the breakfast was ready and he would sit on the veranda and we would sit inside. Then it would depend upon the tide. The tide effects your day. If the tide was in, we would go crabbing and if the tide was out, we would play. And there was a swim usually. Now I like to swim when it is almost in. And what you do at the beach hut really does just depend on the day. If it is windy, you fly a kite, if it is not windy, you play another game. But the possibilities are endless. People say what do you do all day? And you think... it's hard to explain. But the possibilities are just endless".

She says that one of the advantages of being at the beach hut is that her children connect into their family beach routines. She tells me that they are:

> "not all down here sitting on their mobiles. It is fantastic! And they don't miss it. They don't even talk about it. They come down here and off they go. I have got two canoes and we go off and go around the pier and we are knackered, and have to float back".

Steph's recollection of a beach hut day during childhood involved a variety of activities and playing with other children:

> "We would go and put the lobster net out in the morning. I love lobster. Whenever we caught one we would put it in the pot and have it for lunch. We had a fibre-glass boat that was usually kept in the hut. It was always first thing out and last thing into the hut. And next door, Will's family had surf boards and a windsurf stored in the roof.
>
> We were mainly summer hut people. In the summer holidays everyday was a beach day. Whichever parent wasn't working at the time would bring my sister and I down. It was a given that we were here, rain or shine. And in that five-minutes of brightness everyone would tear into the water and then come back, get warm and have something to eat. There would always be someone here, and if not your friends' then you would

play with whoever was here on the day. You would not know people's names it was just friendly and social".

As an adult, her activities in a typical day at the hut are partly functional and partly about play and pleasure:

"I open up the windows, put the chairs and tables outside, get the water and then we have a breakfast — whether it is the full English, bacon roll or sausage roll. I drink tea. I have always got a book or a magazine on the go. I get on the beach, play tennis, rounders and go swimming briefly. I don't stay in like I used to because it is just too chilly now".

She explains that her children have different interests and do not engage in beach hut activities and traditions in the same way that she did as a child:

"This summer we have only been here a few times. My kids are teenagers and have discovered wakeboarding, which is more of an activity and we go down to St Oysth. And if I say 'let's go to the beach' to my kids and they always say 'can I bring somebody?' They are much less likely to just join-in with the other kids on the beach".

BEACH HUT FOOD

When people tell me about their routines, activities and rituals, they often talk about the food they bring, cook and consume at the hut. Eating is a central part of the beach hut experience and meals are planned in advance, anticipated and savoured. Often people start the day with a full English cooked breakfast or bacon sandwiches. Breakfast is eaten outside the hut and is washed down by endless cups of tea. Lunch time and evening barbecues are frequently mentioned accompanied by a few glasses of wine or a beer or two, enjoyed while sitting in the sun. I hear about elaborate picnics with different people bringing more than enough to share with the group. For some, meals are informal, haphazard and makeshift, and for others the cooking at the hut is one of its many pleasures.

Sarah tells me:

> "We just grab all our left-overs from the cupboard and fridge and bring them here. And it always tastes so much nicer down here. In the summer one of our favourite things is staying in the evening. We come down in the afternoon and bring some fresh fish and sit here until just before dark and have a glass of wine".

Jemima also really enjoys cooking in the hut:

> "I have got a boat cooker here with two rings, an oven and a grill which is pure luxury. I used to do a lot of camping and we have got a boat and I often cook on two rings. I don't think anything is beyond the realm of possibility. I often do a steak or a curry or something like that — quite basic food. Part of the fun of cooking at the hut is being creative. And I keep

mine well stocked with food and drink. There are
always a few bottles of gin and a few beers".

Catherine and George tell me beach hut food should be
easy to prepare. Sometimes they bring salads from home
but they also really enjoy cooking bacon and sausages in
the huts. Both particularly associate the smell of frying
bacon with a day at the beach hut. Catherine tells me that
they really appreciate simple food and drink when they are
the hut:

> "Tea tastes nicer here. I don't know why. Perhaps the
> water is different. It always tastes good — I love it".

Several people remember helping their mothers to prepare
a full Sunday lunch in the beach hut in the 1940s and 1950s.
Two people recollect helping to peel potatoes and prepare
vegetables outside the hut and several talked about the
Sunday lunch being cooked in a hut while the family
played on the beach. Some people still like to cook big
meals at the hut. Rebecca says:

> "Mum uses her hut for entertaining, for having
> breakfast, for cooking supper and staring at the sea.
> She uses it year-round".

Lynette she tells me that her family ate Christmas dinner
at the hut. This culinary feat was made possible with a bit
of preparation in advance and benefited from her hut being
less than five minutes from her home:

"Christmas was amazing. Rebecca and I came the day before and we put up all the Christmas decorations and brought in another table so it was like a refectory table. There were 11 of us for lunch and that was fantastic. Once we were sat, we couldn't move around so the people at that end were doing all the serving. We cooked the turkey and prepared the vegetables in the house and then we cooked all the vegetables and did the gravy here. And we had it quite late and people who had an earlier Christmas dinner were walking by and looking surprised".

The people I interview on the Walings, High Wall and The Leas have huts which are not close to the kiosks or the shops. They tell me that one of the attractions of having a hut at Frinton is the lack of commercialisation encountered in other resorts. For many, an important part of their hut routine is a walk to buy ice creams. These excursions are planned, anticipated, and involve some effort. In Chapter 3 *PLACE,* I mention the local furore in 2020 when someone starts to sell refreshments at the top of the slope to The Leas. Most hut owners in this area continue with their long held family traditions of a trek to Walton or Connaught Avenue ignoring the refreshments on sale close by. The ice cream seller trades intermittently during the summer of 2021 and 2022, but appears to get little business. By the end of the summer he has gone... perhaps to trade somewhere more lucrative than this cliff-top spot.

When I talk to people about a day at the hut no one mentions visiting pubs or restaurants. Food is brought from home, from local shops or from take-aways and then consumed outside the hut with a view of the sea. One tradition shared by many is a meal of take-away fish and chips at the end of the day which involves a ritual excursion.

Jenny, Geoff and Amy combine all the beach hut food traditions into a day of indulgence:

> "When we come as a family, we almost always have bacon sandwiches and stay until late and someone will go up and get fish and chips".

Amy interjects:

> "and a we have a picnic at lunchtime! The whole day revolves around food".

AT THE END OF THE DAY

Essentially a day at the beach hut is all about having time to relax, the luxury of having time away from mundane chores and responsibilities, and to enjoy the present. There is a particular way of beach hutting encompassing social rituals, creativity and play. Beach hut people take pleasure in the moment, and in simple things like eating picnics and bacon sandwiches, reading a good book, collecting shells and spending time with family and friends. At the beach hut relaxation is often an active process. Cups of tea are made and consumed; ice cream and toilet excursions are planned; chairs carried, sand castles shaped, discussed and reworked.

As the day progresses castles become sand villages, children become mermaids — half buried in the sand and with sculpted sandy tails — buckets of water are carried up and down the beach, balls thrown and caught. As the beach day ends, mugs are washed, chairs packed, castles are jumped upon or washed away by the incoming tide, children are dried and clothed, towels folded and huts locked. The beach hut forms the backdrop to a day at the beach. A world where leisure and play are fundamental and where the day-to-day routines and worries become trivial.

THINGS CARRIED FROM A BEACH HUT

A crumpled book
A bag full of rubbish
Sandy damp towels
A deflated rubber dinghy
A handful of shells
A sleeping child
A unused mobile phone
A light heart
Tingling skin
The taste of salt

9 — MEMORIES

Like many English resorts, Frinton and Walton thrive on tradition and nostalgia. Shops and kiosks sell beach toys that have changed little over the years; brightly coloured plastic buckets and spades, beach-balls and crabbing kits. Traditional seaside treats are available at ice cream parlours, tea-rooms, and fish and chip take-aways. The combination of resort infrastructure, seaside refreshments and long-established beach activities stir up recollections of childhood, and a time when life was less complicated. The hut is a place to make memories and remember, and this is reflected in names such as *Forget Me Not, Making Memories*, and *Norvic Memories*. A day at the beach hut is not just about being in the here and now, but it is also an

(*above*) Lock's family birthday celebration, High Wall

opportunity to journey back through time and to reminisce.

People share beach hut recollections from their childhood. Sue remembers long pleasurable summers at the hut:

> "You can transport yourself when you are here. I have got loads of special memories of being with everybody. All the family and lots of different people, sitting on the steps and laughing and enjoying being here. Everyday was a special day when we came down".

Most people have photographs of family members enjoying a day at the beach hut. These pictures are cherished and are often on display or kept in albums in the hut. They are brought to my attention and used to illustrate stories of past experiences and memories at the hut. I see pictures of big family gatherings and hear about parents, siblings, children and grandchildren in years gone by.

CHILDHOOD HOLIDAYS

Karen reflects upon her childhood experiences in a rented beach hut with her family:

> "Well, you see the story is that I was born in the early 1950s and we never went anywhere else for our summer holiday. My father booked the same two weeks in June every year and we always used to come to Walton or Frinton. Every single year. And we loved

it, we absolutely loved it, because the beach was so lovely. And in those days, you would have to fight for space on the sand. Not like now where you can sometimes have a whole beach to yourself.

And it was safe. We used to walk the length of the prom on our own and go to the pier and spend our pocket money and what have you. And in those days, it was very easy to rent a bungalow or a property. So, my father would get an estate agent locally to find one in Frinton or Walton, and at the same time rent a beach hut for the two weeks.

I loved being in the beach hut with my mum whilst she made sandwiches and things. And it was lovely to be able to get changed in the beach huts, to have some privacy in the middle of everybody. I always said when I was a little girl 'oh please buy a beach hut so that we can have one of our own and we can keep our things in it'. And my father would say 'oh no, no, no, it wouldn't be worth the expense because we wouldn't get enough use out of it'".

Karen treasures these childhood memories at the beach hut and continues to dream about owning one through her adult life.

A SENSE OF ADVENTURE

Sue recollects the sense of adventure and freedom that she had as a child when she spent a day at the beach:

"I remember walking right out on those days when the tide goes out a long, long way. You know, those days when there is a very high tide followed by a very low tide. And we would walk out and there would be islands of sand. With lots of little rivers between them and my mum would sit up on the balcony and just watch us. And I can remember that we would always have to wear red so that she could see us. And she would wave and we would wave to her to show her that we were safe. Because we were quite young — even at six or seven we would be wandering off down there".

Steph alludes to the freedom to do things that felt slightly dangerous at the beach hut:

"When we were kids there were rafts. That was where we learned to dive. They were fantastic and we learned to swim here and we would dive and mess around. There used to be one of those very high diving boards, one of the old wooden ones with a ladder on the side. It was about five beaches down. And it was not far short of the height of a house. And you would swim out to it. The ladder often had rungs missing — and you would throw yourself off the top. And I can remember doing that when it was quite shallow And I am surprised we didn't break a leg because there was no water".

Emma tells me that she and her siblings used to regularly row out to sea in their blow-up boat:

"We would see how far we could row out before the beach patrol came to tell us to go back. We would do it a couple of times a month and see how far we could get. We would say 'I wonder if we can get the yellow man to come out?'... because the rescue boat was yellow".

These accounts and many more are about the beach as a place to explore, to play and to be adventurous.

CAMARADERIE AND BEACH GAMES

People reminisce about camaraderie within the beach hut community. At the Southcliff huts, Richard shares nostalgic memories, about friendships, formal beach games and families socialising together well into the evening in the 1950s. He grew up in the local area and his family had a beach hut throughout his childhood:

"Well, we used to have a six-week summer holiday and we would be down here all of the time. That was our holiday. I think my dad would have a week off and we would go day-tripping to London. But most of our holiday was here. We used to meet different people that came every year and we would meet children from other beach huts at different times over the six weeks. We really loved it. We had great fun and often if the tide was low at the end of the day there would be big cricket matches on the sand. And we all played because we all knew each other. We used to have

massive games of rounders with everybody joining in
and there were competitions organised by the Council.

They used to have lights along the promenade and
we'd stay until 10 o'clock and everyone had little gas
lights in their huts. It seemed more crowded then. A
lot more people came. There were fewer huts but
more people".

Ruth is Richard's beach hut neighbour and they have
known each other since they were children. She recollects
that same period in the 1950s and early 1960s

"We used to have sports day here when the tide was out.
I think it was sponsored by the Daily Mirror and it
happened once a year. It was more of a community in
those days, regular people would be down for the
holidays so it was a real community. You don't get that
same atmosphere and friendliness now".

Further round at The Leas, Sue recalls big groups of people
enjoying beach hut games together in the late 1960s and
early 1970s:

"There were beach hut games. My dad was one of the
organisers. He would get all the kids and there would
be obstacle courses and rounders. It was a really big
thing and it would go right into the evening. I am sure
that the coastguards were involved and they would
come down and we would have fires on the beach. And

the adults would get drunk and the kids would be playing into the night".

In Frinton in the huts on Low Wall, Steph recollects the 1970s:

"There were never organised games here but a few people would start playing and then all the parents would get involved. At the end of the day — you didn't know anyone's name but you all played together and had just had a nice day".

Emmas recalls informal friendships made on the beach outside the family hut at Eastcliff during her childhood in the 1980s. Her children developed similar beachhut friendships:

"Every summer we would go down to the beach and every summer there was a boy at another beach hut called Dean. I don't know his surname and don't know anything about him but we used to play every year. He was the same age as me and we didn't have inflatables or surfboards or anything like that. We would be digging in the sand and swimming all day. We didn't stay in touch. We weren't pen pals, but every year we were so glad to see each other. And we saw the same families year in and year out. And they were the people who we got to know and played with.

And when my oldest son was little, he had the same type of friendship with a family about six beach huts down from ours. They only saw each other at the beach but when they were here, they played together constantly".

COMMUNITY EVENTS

Some beach huts continue to be used as a base for community games and activities. Emma teaches in a local primary school, and over the years has organised beach games and activities from her hut:

> "I have run school trips and events down at our beach hut. Once the RNLI did a beach safety course for 60 children on the beach outside the hut. Another time we hired a sports coach to run beach sports for the kids. When I was a Beaver leader the Cubs always had their end of year ceremony at the beach hut. Also, in the past I have organised a 'toddle-waddle' on the beach to raise money for our local Barnardo's mother and toddler group. During Covid the beach hut has been useful. One of my son's plays for Clacton F.C. and when the football presentation was cancelled this year, we decided to invite them all down at the beach hut instead for the day".

Mary tells me that her beach hut has been the base for Church events and barbecues. Terry holds parties for the resident's association of his block of flats at his hut. Alex (from Birch Hall Adventures) has organised games on the beach in front of his family hut during Cadet Week at the local sailing club (Walton and Frinton Yacht Club).

BIRTHDAYS AND FAMILY GATHERINGS

Amy and her family hold an annual beach hut party:

> "Mum has a friend with a birthday in August and every
> year we come up for that. That's an annual tradition.
> All the children have been coming down here for years
> and as they have got older, they have just kept coming
> down. Most years there are probably 20-25 of us with
> boyfriends and girlfriends. So that is one of our
> traditions. It is on the 13th of August and it doesn't
> matter what day of the week — rain or shine, we all
> come down. And there are loads of us and we just take
> over this bit of the beach. There is always a cake!"

Along similar lines, Helen remembers one of her son's
birthdays:

> "We invited lots of our friends down and they all brought
> their children and we had a party. There were just so
> many of us we just took over the whole beach. It was
> brilliant. And we swam and we went on the bodyboards.
> Michael brought his canoe down and we have got lovely
> photos of them digging little holes and filling them up
> with water and finding things. It was just lovely".

Emma used to regularly hold birthday parties at the hut:

> "My children's birthdays are all in the summer. When
> they were 4 or 5 years old, we would have pirate
> parties. They children would dress as pirates and we

Birthday celebration, The Leas

would make a pirate ship in the sand with a gangplank
and they would hunt for treasure".

Olivia also talks about regular family gatherings at the hut,
recalling one particularly memorable day in 2020 when
the whole family had visited together.

> "As the grandchildren get a bit older and they can really
> enjoy a day on the beach. The little ones' love burying
> their dad in the sand. And there was a day last year
> when all the kids had come, and it was so hot, and
> everyone was on the beach, and we were all drinking
> champagne. Well not the grandchildren — they were
> playing! All the adults had champagne and we had lots
> of food and it was a perfect day, beautiful weather".

Huts are often used as a venue for celebrations and can be
seen decked out with balloons and Happy Birthday
banners. Some of the rental huts can be hired out together
and in the summer larger parties are often held in the
space in front of several adjoining huts. Parties spill out
from the hut and onto the beach and both Helen and Amy
talk about the pleasure in having a sense that they take
over the beach when they hold a party at the hut.

INCIDENTS

Some people recollect a specific day which was different from
their regular experiences of beach hut life. Ruth remembers
a bomb incident on a visit to the hut during her childhood:

"One day the police and the army came and asked us to move down to the beach. Fortunately, the tide was out and we all went down onto the rafts because we didn't know what was happening. There was a bomb at the back and they had to set it off! That was quite something, with all of us still down on the beach when the bomb exploded. If it happened now the whole area would have been evacuated, but all we had to do then was to go down onto the beach. It was quite a big explosion and really it left a big old crater at the back there. There are so many memories of times with the family but that is an unusual one".

Catherine and George's hut is located at the top of steep concrete steps on High Wall in Frinton. George recollects an incident that occurred before he built a veranda:

"We were sitting up on these chairs on the slope and our friends were here. We were chatting for ages and I was laughing so much that my chair tipped over. I fell down the steps and broke the top of my femur. It was quite a serious break. I couldn't move.

Luckily a couple were walking by and helped. She was a retired nurse and he was a retired policeman and had first aid experience. And so, he went up to the top to ring and then wait for the ambulance and she stayed looking after me. It took a long while for the ambulance to get here. No one had the code for the nearest gates. There was a PSO here but no one had been notified of that month's code. In the end they came along the promenade from Walton and then had to reverse from the toilets at the corner. We waited for over an hour and a half down here.

It didn't put us off. We are still coming and that is why I built the veranda... to stop us from rolling down the steps!"

Further down the beach Maureen and Phillip recall an unpleasant experience at their hut a few years before when they were on their own in the early evening:

"There were not many people around and there were five or six youngsters on the beach being a bit leary. One of them came up and wanted to borrow my towel. I was wary and he became aggressive and just took it. Then several of them got up onto the roof and they started running up and down. It was horrible and they were all around us... some on the roof and some around here. They tried to get into the hut and we wouldn't let them in and it became nasty and frighting. Fortunately, another couple came to assist us, but when the youths left they said 'we are coming back you know' and we were worried that they would smash up the hut. It was really difficult because this is our little paradise we love it so much and it felt like that paradise had been broken".

Steph recollects the day in 2019 when the beach was closed due to toxic fumes from an algal bloom in the sea:

> "The weather had been really hot and the sea had been really still for a few days. Lots of people were on the beach and I think it was a doctor who noticed that people were having difficulty breathing and they were coughing and wheezing when they came out of the sea. And they called out the police and the fire service. It seemed to start in this part of the beach and then because of the tide it moved towards Walton and then later it moved to in Holland-on-Sea. It seemed to affect different parts of the beach. My friend scuba dives and he was affected, but it didn't affect other friends who were on the beach in Walton".

The incident made it to the national newspapers, leading to a police warning people not to go into the water over the Bank Holiday weekend, when temperatures reached 32 degrees. The huts were still busy over the weekend, but families with children stayed away and the beach was unusually empty.

REMEMBRANCE

Several people explain that they have developed deepening attachments to their huts, the beach and the surrounding area. Beach huts form an important part of childhood holiday experiences for many and the hut has become a place to remember and commemorate family members who have died, particularly parent and grandparents. Karen says:

> "My parents loved Frinton, and they loved having a walk down from the hut, sitting in the tiny little church at the end of Connaught Avenue and just looking at things. They used to love sitting in the memorial garden in the back. When they died, we got permission to scatter their ashes there and so we always go and visit them when we are down. It is nice because it was their favourite place, and they were always happy to come here for their holidays and days out, year after year. They never bothered with anywhere else because my father used to say 'I can't think of anywhere as good'".

Sue explains that visiting her hut feels like she is carrying on her family tradition:

> "It makes me think that my family is still here. My parents passed away ages ago. But I can still feel their presence here. There are some things in the beach hut that were rescued from the old one. So, I still have my dad's mug".

Sarah has a similar sense that owning and being in her hut is a way of maintaining family customs and memories:

> "When my mum and dad first found this place to hire, my mum absolutely loved it. She was born abroad and

had travelled around a lot as a child. She loves England and she always wanted to have a beach hut. I think that is why we wanted to buy it and to take it over. I wanted to remember her".

Helen explains how the family commemorated her father at the hut:

"Dad died on New Year's Eve and the following year we all came down in our winter coats and we brought sloe gin to drink, to toast him, because it is such a special place for us all".

Emma is planning an annual beach hut get together to commemorate her mum:

"We have said that every year we will spend a day together at the beach and we will have all the children together in mum's memory. I think it will become an annual thing".

Richard rebuilt his hut for his sister when she had cancer:

"The new hut was for her really. She is dead now but my brother-in-law still comes down here. I have some nice memories of my sister and brother-in-law sitting inside and also my wife who died in 2010. I have got photos of her here. I have even got pictures of my dad sitting on the prom. I have loads of memories here".

John stopped visiting his hut for a few years after his wife died:

"My wife's parents always came to Frinton and we used to come with them and we always enjoyed that. When they passed-on we inherited some money and we bought the hut. We used it a lot but then my wife passed four years ago and I stopped coming".

He has recently started to visit again with his friend Betty:

"Well, he has started to visit more now that he has met me. We came down several times last year and we have just started to come again this year. We painted it all up last year and we are planning to use it a bit more now".

Susan says it was difficult to make the decision to replace her grandfather's hut:

"because it evoked so many strong memories. My grandparents died in 1976 and my father took it over and he died in 1985. I took it over when my mum died in 1992. My grandfather was a painter/decorator/builder in the area and he had it probably for 75-80 years. I don't know the exact date, but it was always on this site. In those days the hut was dismantled each year and grandad would come along with his handcart and they all went up onto the carpark for the winter. Before the sea wall was built, they took them down at the end of the summer each year. When we were children there were railings and it was more exposed to the sea and the storms.

And when my grandad and dad were here, they kept it in good condition. My husband and I are not handy people and my brother is not a handy person either so we just held it together with nails really. And every year we would pack it up for the winter and hope when we reopened it that it would open properly and be alright. It took a long while to replace it because there was so much emotion bound up with the old hut".

Like Helen and Anne in Chapter 5 *STYLE*, she is reluctant to change the colour of the hut:

"The hut has to be green because grandad always had it green. He always had it a darker green, but over the years I have toned it down a bit so that we have got the more of a pastel green now. It wasn't ever stained".

In September 2022, I notice that there are several laminated birthday cards attached to the hut *Daddy's Girls*. A closer look leads to the realisation that this is a memorial to a hut owner and that the family had shared a posthumous 77th birthday at the hut. The hut has become a significant place for family and friends to celebrate, reflect and remember. The cards displayed on the front of the hut included messages about loss and love. One card says that they sang Happy Birthday:

"Hope you could hear us.Happy heavenly birthday Dad".

A BOX FULL OF MEMORIES

Huts are places for remembrance but also places where people can spend special days and amass memories for the future. Anna explains the importance of memory-making and refers to the significance of her own childhood reminiscences of the family hut in Mersey:

> "My childhood memories at the hut were just about spending time with my cousins. It is very much who you spend your time with at the hut. I got into real scrapes as a child. I remember falling off one of the floating pontoons while I was crabbing and a lady scooping me out with a fishing net. It is about those sort of memories. And I think it is very much about who you get to spend your time with. My daughter is an only child and we bought a hut because we want to create a space where she can make lots of memories with her cousins and her friends. I want her to have lots of childhood memories of being at the beach".

The recollections shared in this chapter reinforce the idea that the hut is much more than its physical structure. Huts can spark reminiscences of siblings, partners, parents and grandparents. For many, spending time at the hut powerfully reconnects people to experiences and feelings from their childhood. The hut is a time-machine, a receptacle for precious memories which can be reawakened and reiterated during each visit. I reflect on my own experience and realise that I don't have a physical space

where I can connect with previous generations of my family.
Sure, I have photographs and other small mementos, but
my recollection of my childhood home and my
grandparents' homes have become blurred over time. I like
the idea of beach hut time-travelling, of walking into a
small space and being enveloped in powerful memories of
childhood. I wonder what it would be like to experience
that intensity of feelings, to enter a place where I could be
emotionally engaged and perhaps be overwhelmed by the
past. I realise it is too late for me now and feel a sense of
envy of people who have a space where they can reconnect
to other times and to people who are no longer here. Finally,
I am starting to develop a deeper understanding of the
appeal of a beach hut.

10 — STORIES

Conversation and storytelling are an important part of beach hut life. This is reflected in many hut names such as *Once upon a tide, Linger Longer, Chatterbox* and *'Jabbas' The Hutch;* and the frequent associations with literature and film which were identified in Chapter 7 *NAMING.* The hut is a convivial place, people slow down and take the time to talk.

Several stories in the previous chapter are tinged with sadness as people reminisce about relatives and friends who are integral to their joyful memories of the past but are no longer alive. Some people reflect upon the pleasures and challenges of bringing elderly relatives to the beach. They recall the complicated logistics involved in manoeuvring wheelchairs and mobility scooters to the hut, the toilets and

(above) John and Louisa Beale, Frinton.

down onto the beach. These tales are accompanied by tears and laughter as loved ones are recollected fondly. In his book *The Storytelling Animal — How stories make us human*, Jonathan Gottschall says that storytelling is a process of connection, a kind of "social glue that brings people together around common values" (2012:28). This process is apparent in stories shared at the beach hut as people connect and recollect, with friends, family and beach hut neighbours. Anecdotes are shared, interrogated and reworked for me as we sit chatting outside people's huts drinking tea and watching the sea. Often beach hut stories merge into tales of other places, other times and other people. They loosely knit together into winding narratives which coalesce and have a collective resonance.

Beach hut tales are jointly crafted and are part of the ongoing process of experiencing and being at the hut. Some common themes are apparent in the previous chapter where people share memories of childhood holidays, parties and community events, and the beach hut as a place for remembrance. Stories develop in conversation as hut owners encounter one another and create collective understandings and appreciation of the vagaries and delights of the hut. These shared tales bond people together and create a sense of belonging within a community.

CREATING STORIES

One common thread that I haven't explored so far are the tales about the previous owners of huts. Often the new beach hut owner has never actually met their predecessors, however many share detailed accounts about them. These stories are imagined, pieced together from the recollections of beach hut neighbours, brief meetings during the sale process and the artifacts left in the hut. So, for example Karen tells me about 'Mr Bejam' who previously owned her hut. She can't remember his name but knows he used to own a chain of food shops called Bejam and that he sold them off to another chain called Iceland. She has never met him but tells me:

"Well, Mr Bejam, or whatever his proper name is, had a lot of property in Frinton and Walton and owned loads of huts. Apparently, he was very kind to his employees back in the day and used to let them come down and have holidays here and use the huts. But he had sold all of them off, since he was no longer involved with the business... except this one. I suppose he kept it for his family, but the chap who was selling it said he could only remember the family visiting once. Apparently, his son came down with his girlfriend because she wanted to see what a beach hut was like. This chap opened it up for them and she looked inside and then off they went. They didn't stay... just had a look inside. And apart from that it had been standing here for I don't know how many years doing nothing. And so, Mr Bejam decided to sell it off".

Commonly people construct stories about the previous owners around the things that they leave in their huts.

Lynette previously owned *Dalriada*:

> "I bought this beautiful old hut which had belonged to
> the same family for generations. They were selling it
> because this old man owned it and his wife had died and
> he just couldn't come here because of the memories.
> And the family, the two daughters and he, sold it just as
> it was. I inherited some of the plates that were in there".

She kept the plates and put them on display after she
renovated the hut. The plates provide a link to the huts past
and to people she has never met.

Sarah and Martin rented *The Waves* for many years
before they bought it. Martin shows me around:

> "Lots of things in the hut are from the previous owner.
> She left quite a bit when she sold it, including all the
> paintings. It is interesting because she has quite a lot
> of French pictures and things and I am wondering if
> she had some connection with France".

They are both pleased to have inherited her memorabilia
because it is an important part of their own experience of
the hut and creates a sense of history. Sarah shows me the
previous owner's log book:

> "This is one that I like. The last Sunday in March
> 2007 — that is quite early on in the year isn't it. 'After
> spending a night at the hut woken up at 6.30 a.m. by a
> hut warden saying 'Get Out' and assuming that we

don't own it. It was pretty horrible. Then he saw the keys and realised that we owned it. If I ever do that again I will secure the locks from the outside and climb in through the window'.

We bought the hut later that year in September 2007. We didn't write anything in the log until we owned the hut because we felt it was hers. When we moved in my mum bought a special book for us so we could continue the tradition".

When Sarah sells the hut in 2021, she decides to leave the previous owners log book in the hut but they keep their own log book because it includes their recollections of special days and experiences including time spent with her parents at the hut when they were in their late 80s.

STORYTELLING

Beach hut memories are constructed in particular family and social contexts, and often told in conversation. These shared reminiscences involve different family members chipping in to add another detail or to reinforce a particular phrase or saying. The tale is alive, and each telling is unique because it involves the interplay of recollections, with decisions made about where to place emphasis, where to laugh, where to pause and when to have another slice of cake. People talk at the same time, sometimes finishing one anothers sentences, other times seeking clarification or agreement. The conversation below provides an example.

It is told by two sisters, Helen and Anne and their guest Mavis, who is an old family friend. It is accompanied by tea, cake and lots of laughter:

> "I was often invited here with my late husband. We would get a phone call saying 'we are off to the beach' and they would say 'do you fancy coming?' And I would say 'you can't keep me away' and we would come down and bring a picnic and swimmers ...." (Mavis).

> "Yeah, you would bring your swimmers and sit and watch the world go by. Dad and Richard used to sit out the front with their brown tummies and their glass of wine..." (Helen).

> "... Like a proper farmer. And Mary and myself would sit round this corner out of the wind and ..." (Mavis).

> "And natter..." (Helen).

> "And natter... We would knit and natter really". (Mavis)

> "Dad, used to sit there the first thing he would say is 'nice here innit'" (Anne).

> "Yes, he always said that" (Helen).

> "And then he used to say (*in a Punch and Judy voice*) 'that's the way to do it'..."(Anne).

> "... He would sit there with his brown tummy and he would say 'nice here innit'..." (Helen).

"... So, it was our parents and Mavis, a friend of mum and dad, and her husband .... everyone would come down wouldn't they.... (Helen).

"Yeah, and we used to bring our grandparents down as well, when they were elderly..." (Anne).

"Every weekend we would bring a picnic. Bring the lunch. Cook something on the stove. And it was always something like quiche and potatoes and salad — a proper little lunch wasn't it. And a glass of wine..." (Helen).

"... and cake..."(Anne — *Pauses to bite into a slice of cake*).

"... and cake... We would just sit here and watch the world go by — just relaxing. And then the grandchildren all came along and so they would come down. We have got such happy memories of them all coming down here. Being with mum and dad and the grandparents..." (Helen).

"... And the children's birthday parties. They used to have them down here." (Mavis).

"Yes. My son's birthday parties and there would be dozens of us taking over the beach....We gave him a thunderstorm one year. His friends all came down for a party and there must have been nine or ten of us and the heavens opened. There was a huge thunderstorm and we all had to hide inside the hut. And we had the front open and it was amazing. There was thunder, lightning on the sea and water was just running down the beach. And then when it was all over they just ran around in it because it was so exciting. You know it was amazing and they just loved it"(Helen).

"What about them on their scooters?" (Anne).

"... Oh yes! The kids when they were small, they used to bring their scooters down. And they used to come down the slope at top speed on their scooters. Scaring the life out of me... But they loved it from when they were tiny babies. My husband he used to lay on that wall and go to sleep and I have got a picture of one of the children lying on his tummy. He is on his back and he has got one of the children on his tummy asleep on that wall... And there is a lovely photo of grandma — great grandma, isn't there. Holding one of the children at the hut... And then we would let people like the WI (Women's Institute) come down because mum belonged to the WI and they would all come down and have an evening here..." (Helen).

"Yes. We used to come down with the WI in the evenings. A lot of them were elderly... and we would bring them all down and there would be a dozen or so of us. We would play boules and go for a paddle and I would drive up to the chip shop and get fish and chips. Then we would sit out here and eat fish and chips and

go home when it got dark. It was lovely..."
(Mavis — *Long pause as everyone looks out to sea).*

"Yes. It was lovely. The evenings are lovely down here. And great grandma, she was elderly but every time she came — Dad would take her down to the beach slowly and she would hitch up her skirt or dress..." (Helen).

"... And take her stockings off..." (Anne).

"... take her stockings off. And she would always walk along in the water because she thought it was good for her feet. So, he would walk his mother along the water with me.... and it was lovely" (Helen).

"Grandma and grandad were 93 when they died and they were still coming down here" (Anne).

"Yes. It was not so difficult because we are next to the slope and the toilets. And we used to have a key to the gate and drive them down because they were elderly and drop them off here and then take the car back up. And then when the children were young in the afternoon, we would leave the oldies here and we would all walk along to Walton and get an ice cream. We would have the babies in the push chairs and as they grew older they would go on their scooters. And we would walk right along the front — right to Walton pier and then walk all the way back again. And it was lovely" (Helen).

"And for our grandad we used to wrap an ice cream up

in newspaper or a towel or something and try and get back here as fast as we could so that he could have his ice cream" (Anne).

"... And then when mum had had her stroke, we would push her wheelchair down the slope to the beach, wouldn't we... And then grandad would come down here in a wheelchair after grandma had died. Just such happy memories. And my children when they grew up, they used to love to bring their friends here. When they could drive, they would say 'oh can we have the hut'. And they would bring their friends down. Big games of cricket on the beach and it was just lovely.... It is all happy memories because it is so special" (Helen).

"It just full of memories"... (Anne — *long pause*).

"Our beach hut is full of memories ....I walk down that slope and the emotions just overwhelm me" (Helen — *long pause... we all drink tea*).

As I listen to this story, I think about the way in which the three women narrate and share their experiences. It brings to mind the idea of *'living-stories'* (Molbjerg Jorgensen, 2017) which ripen with each telling. The three women create a story which is a distillation of their experiences and an experience in itself. It is woven together as they talk, laugh, eat cake and drink tea in the sun. Their story is relational and spontaneous; ideas are sparked by one speaker and taken forward by another. Sometimes they finish one anothers sentences and other times they repeat ideas to reinforce their importance. This is a unique telling of a story that reflects the dynamics between these three women on that particular day as they share their tale with me, a stranger.

LIFE STORY

Sometimes the beach hut is the setting or the catalyst for an important event. As I am collecting stories for this book, I hear about Steph who married the boy from the beach hut next door. I want to hear the story first-hand and we agree to meet one evening in late September. It has been raining during the day and the beach is empty. The air is cool, it is drizzling and it feels like the summer is over. As I arrive at the hut the sun emerges and there is an improbably vivid rainbow arching across the sea. We don't trust the weather and sit inside the hut drinking a cup of tea and just watching as the rainbow disappears and the weather clears. The early evening sky is beautiful, initially a grey blue with big billowing white clouds on the horizon. Then the sun starts to set, tinging the clouds pale pink and orange, and darkening the sky to deep blue. The first half hour of our meeting is spent watching sky and sea, with sporadic talking about the beautiful view and the feelings it evokes. We relax and reflect. On the second cup of tea Steph starts to tell me about spending summer holidays at the beach hut during her childhood. She has many memories of that time and used to spend hours playing with Will, the boy in the beach hut next door.

"My gran used to say Will was like my shadow on the beach. Wherever I went he was always right behind me. Whether it was digging, or swimming or crabbing he was always two feet behind. We were the youngest — his brothers and my sisters are older. We were always the babies and we used to just wander off by ourselves. We both remembered shrimping in the evening — we used to collect bucket loads of them".

She talks about the adventures they had... going out in her father's small boat to put down lobster pots, jumping off the rafts and playing with lots of other children:

"Then we sold the hut when I was 11 and so I stopped seeing him regularly. And I really didn't know him during his teenage years and don't have many memories of visiting the hut then. When I did occasionally visit, we didn't spend time together as he was with his mates. He says he does not remember me coming here when we were teenagers".

They reconnected in their late 20s when she was visiting her parents:

"Mum said 'Will's around, why don't you go out for a drink?' So we went out for a few drinks and the rest is history. When I proposed to Will, I had already booked the church and the vicar!"

She shows me a picture of the two of them on the beach

162

together during their childhood at a time when both families regularly visited their huts:

> "That picture was all over the place at my wedding. It is important and shows us having fun when we were kids and also shows the length of time, we have known each other".

The beach hut has a special place in their shared histories and Will's family still own a hut which means that they can visit regularly:

> "On one of our early anniversaries, he borrowed a picnic hamper from someone and made all my favourite sandwiches. And we came down here and had this glorious picnic. We spent the evening sitting, and it was beautiful and about as quiet as it is now. It was just perfect. He always says as soon as he brings me down here, he can see all my troubles have gone. My shoulders relax. I really feel that this is my place. And he is so pleased that he has got this hut that he can share with me".

The slow start to Steph's story reflects and respects the spectacular weather conditions that we experience from the hut. The life story is paused for the light show as the weather clears and the sun starts to set. The delay in the start of the story illustrates the way that being at the hut can provide a very different perspective. We move into beach hut time as we pause to reflect, watch and just enjoy.

Steph, Grandma and Natalie, Low Wall

BEACH HUT TALES

Beach hut stories are told within a specific place and community and illustrate slices of day-to-day life. They are small, ordinary tales about people's lives but they have a richness and resonate with me. These are not my stories but I can relate to them because they reflect the tales told within my own family. I feel a growing connection with beach hut people because their stories touch upon our common emotions and feelings.

These stories are told in the place where they are created and constantly refer to that setting. They retell past events, consolidate memories and give them shape. Each time they are told, they are reworked and reconfigured to reflect the teller's mood, or the listener's interest. Storytelling enables people to identify what is important to them and to express their beach hut identity. They convey a beach hut 'literacy' and include tips and warnings to other hut owners; knowledge about the best way to weather-proof huts, ideas for cooking; approaches to decorating, year-round activities, and family traditions that support the best days at the beach. Underlying these beach hut tales sit ideas about connection to a place through repeated visits, a sense of familiarity and understanding of a particular part of the beach. Stories impart beach hut savvy.

Nina and Sam outside *Seahorse*, Southcliff

11 — BUSINESSES

The boundaries between business and pleasure are blurred
for most people who rent out beach huts. The people who
rent often choose to spend time visiting their huts with
family and friends when they are not booked by visitors.
Many of these small businesses are run by women from the
local area. 'Walton on the Naze Beach Huts' is located on
Eastcliff, and in 2022 owned 12 rental huts. 'Daisy' and
'Alice' hut rentals are both located on Southcliff and in 2022
each had 11 rental huts. In addition, 'Daisy' beach huts have
a holiday let which is rented through Airbnb. There are also
a growing number of smaller rental businesses most of
whom own two or three huts. The smaller businesses often
manage their huts themselves rather than contracting out
work to local cleaning and maintenance businesses.

LYNETTE

Lynette rents out two huts on Eastcliff and lives locally. In 2019, she tells me:

"We got *Willowbeach* a few years ago when my daughter and I started a little business renting out a caravan at the Willows Caravan Park. We completely renovated it and styled the caravan with a 1950s theme and then we bought the beach hut, continued the 1950s theme and hired the two together. We did it for about two years and were run off our feet. We were making a profit but it was hard work and we decided it was not worth it. We had to pay our site fees for the caravan which were nearly £2,000 and that really ate into our profit . It was too much work... it didn't work out and so we sold the caravan and refocused on the beach huts. The second hut is called *Vitamin Sea*. My daughter ran a B&B for a while, and then she moved away and now I look after these two on my own.

I don't have a website and I don't want to have one. I like to be in touch a bit more really. And people tend to come back. Some other beach hut renters have websites and they often have little key boxes at the side of the hut. In some cases, they don't see the people they are renting to. So, they have no connection with the people who hire the hut. For some people that is lovely but I like to meet the people who rent my huts".

Lynette shows me the hut bookings. It is August, the weather is good and most people have made daily bookings which means that she visits to clean every day:

"There seven days of different people coming which meant seven days of cleaning. Most people leave by 5.30 but some stay until 9.00 in the evening. We normally start at 9:00 in the morning so I will be down at 8:00 the next day. It does not matter how clean they leave it, I still have to go over it. I am quite particular about it. I need to check that they have turned off the gas and emptied the water. Last week I had people in and they had forgotten to empty the water and they had eaten fish and chips inside. It stank. But most people leave it tidy and it normally takes 10-15 minutes to set up.

When people come, they say it is gorgeous. And I ask people to leave it as they found it. I had a terrible time last year when a family booked in for a week and then invited other families to stay with them. After they left, I opened the door, looked in and I said 'oh my God!' It was filthy, rubbish everywhere! Nothing had been washed and all the plates had been piled up with food still stuck in between. The cooker was covered in white fat, everything was covered in grease and food. There were ants everywhere. It was disgusting! It took two of us three hours to clean inside and then I had to wash the cushions. Everything had to be taken out of the hut.

169

I had to wash everything in boiling water and bleach all the surfaces. It took three hours!"

KEVIN AND SOPHIE

Kevin and Sophie are in their 30s and live about an hour away in Sudbury. They have two huts on Southcliff which they rent out throughout the year. When I meet them in May 2021, they are painting the deck. We are in the midst of the Pandemic and emerging from the third lockdown. International travel is restricted and their huts are booked out for the summer. Kevin tells me that he started coming to the huts at Walton when his mum bought one about seven years ago:

"We love the beach here because it is sandy and so flat. It is such a nice place and it always seems so friendly. We love the ones that have decks on them, and are a bit higher up. You don't hear the noise from the front. All you can hear is the sea and you have some privacy. You just see a few dog walkers and a few people in their huts up here.

We bought the first one to rent in 2017 and used some money which I had saved for a house deposit. They seemed like really good value for money. I could see how much they were going up in price each year and renting them is really popular. In 2019 we bought the stripy green and white one along there. We rent both out and use them ourselves when family come down. On days like today when it is not being used it is nice to come down and sit and have a cup of tea.

At the moment people are buying them because they want somewhere to go. For some it is perhaps a status symbol... but it is basically just a shed. There is no water supply, no electricity".

In the rental business the name and décor of the hut is important. When Kevin and Sophie bought their first hut it was brown and they decided to repaint it "Cadbury's purple". Once it was painted, they put an image on Facebook with some ideas for names. The most popular name was *Fruit and Nut Hut*. The other one was already painted in green and white stripes when they bought it:

> "When we were naming it, we thought about things that are green and went down the apple route and called it *Bramley*. In *Fruit and Nut Hut* we have gone for a purple kettle, sugar bowls, cups, cushions and in *Bramley* they are all green. So, there is a little bit of a theme. We have put up bunting, taken pictures of the beach and had them made into canvases. We have been thinking more about design ever since they did that design challenge down on the front. We will probably develop a theme for each of them in the future".

Sophie tells me that they do all the maintenance work themselves. They plan to work on *Bramley* in the winter, replacing the floor and redesigning the kitchen.

"In *Fruit and Nut Hut* we have got the U-seating around the back and you can put the table in the middle. So, you can get everyone around the table if it is a bad day. Whereas *Bramley* has a kitchen on the left-hand side and seating on the right-hand side and there is nowhere to put a table. If you put a table in front of the seating area then you can't get to the kitchen. And you do need a space inside in case it is a rainy day. You can't guarantee the British weather".

I find details of their huts on a beach hut website. In 2021 they charge £45 per day in peak season and £35 out of season for the huts and both huts are both available all year round:

"This year we started getting bookings as soon as we were allowed to open again at the end of April and start of May. In a normal year we might get a couple of bookings around Easter time and then not a lot until May, June, July, August and then a few in September. We do dailies, but we have a few people who book a couple of days in a row. We hire it to an artist several times a year and she has it for a week at a time and just sits up here and paints.

Covid has made a massive difference to the rental market. This summer holiday is booked up. The first part of May was hectic because we were coming out of lockdown and the weather was really good. We are booked up over the summer holidays already".

Kevin and Sophie's huts offer some rental income in the summer and the opportunity to visit throughout the year. Sophie tells me they love to visit in the winter:

> "We come down a lot in December and January as it is nice to have a bathe in the sea and a cup of tea in the hut. I like to read and Kevin might go for a run. I bring my parents down some evenings and we will sit up here, have a cup of coffee maybe get some fish and chips and just relax".

Kevin particularly likes to visit in the early morning before the day trippers arrive

> "If we are not working, we like coming down here for breakfast. We get here, bacon butty, cup of tea. We like to come just to relax — sometimes we walk to Frinton along the seafront".

Sophie and Kevin mix business with pleasure. They enjoy gaining rental income from their huts and like the idea of their huts as an investment, but they also really enjoy being able to spend time at their huts.

NINA

Nina set up a beach hut business with her dad in 2019 and bought her first hut *Ladybird* in row B on Southcliff in January 2020. I speak to her in 2022 and she tells me about renovating her first hut.

"We put up some of the family in a caravan and they came to put on the deck in February half term in torrential rain. And then Covid hit and I came here on Mothers Day, just before lockdown and the deck was done but we hadn't had a chance to paint or do anything inside. We had to stop as we could not travel, but I started my Instagram page to get the communication going because I intended to rent her out. At the end of lockdown, we came down for 10 days and ripped everything out including the old kitchen and fixed the ceiling. Dad is an odd job man so he can do everything and my husband did all the exterior painting. I was responsible for prettying it all up. We launched one week into the summer holidays and overnight we sold out. Because of Covid there was so much uncertainty and so the British seaside had a resurgence".

Spurred on by the success of her first hut she buys two more. The story behind the mural on her second hut 'Seahorse' is shared in Chapter 7 *STYLE*, and reflects her passion for refurbishing and styling beach huts. She has a background in fashion marketing and effervesces with design ideas. Her huts are flamboyant, imaginatively styled and are supported by innovative social media messaging and a professional website. She understands the potential of a good story and uses her website to share information about her journey and aspirations for the hut business:

"My ongoing vision is to create unique, high end, stylish coastal retreats for my guests to kick back and relax, a dream away from daily strains and stresses, to rejuvenate in solitude or with loved ones... making time for ourselves is so important for our mind, body and soul".

Nina and I meet several times in 2022 and it clear that she is exploring a variety of ideas and collaborative opportunities with local photographers and businesses. She markets her beach hut as a backdrop for photoshoots and as a base for charity events. She is also exploring ways of extending the traditionally short beach hut season and has themed one of her huts as the "Little Hut of Horrors" for Halloween bookings. As I get to know Nina better, I discover that developing the hut business has provided a way of forging relationships within her family. She was estranged from her dad when she was a child and did not reconnect with him until recently. The beach hut business provides an opportunity to spend time together on a shared project and to get to know one another better.

As I collect stories for this book, I repeatedly hear anecdotes about the growth in the rental market in Walton and Frinton. Local and national newspapers report on the growing popularity of huts and rising prices. Beach hut rental is seen to be a lucrative business opportunity and there are rumours of huts being rented for £90 per day. However, the tales I hear from the people who actually rent out their huts suggest more caution. I feel unconvinced by oft-mentioned £90 a day rates and decide to check the rental prices in early-September 2021. I check two listing sites — www.huts4hire.co.uk and www.airbnb.co.uk. I discover that in 2021 the daily rates are most commonly in the range of £30-39 off peak and £40-49 during peak season. Weekly rates are usually under £160 both during peak and off-peak season. Some huts are already into their off-peak season. If I want to rent a hut, I can choose from dozens available at locations all along the beach. I check again in September 2022 and discover that day rental rates are very similar to 2021, weekly rental rates have risen slightly and are around £200.

CHALLENGES

The majority of beach hut owners in Walton and Frinton rent their plots from Tendring Council on one-year site licences. The Council's licence conditions have been unchanged for many years which means that the hut owners who decide to develop a rental business have a sense of stability. National and regional press reports on this lucrative market in 2020 and 2021 fuels speculation, and more people purchase and refurbish huts for rental market. The insecurities of the rental business become apparent in early 2022 when rumours start to circulate that renting will be restricted in both resorts. Some of the rental businesses form 'The Tendring Beach Hut Rental Committee' and try to negotiate with the Council. They argue that the beach hut rental provides affordable access to beach huts for locals and visitors, raises the profile of the area as a destination, increases local employment and spending at destination, and improves the appearance and maintenance of huts. The uncertainties about rentals continue throughout 2022 and into 2023 and while it appears that some commercial licences might be available it is not made clear to the rental companies how these might be allocated and what their costs might be.

The ongoing uncertainty presents challenges to the beach hut rental companies. Winter is normally a time when they maintain and renovate their huts, update their websites and start to take bookings for the next season. I check the three main rental companies on 15 February 2023 to see if I will be able to rent a hut for a day at Easter. There are no dates showing. The message on the 'Alice Beach Huts' website:

> "As soon as we know (and at the moment we don't even know WHEN we'll know) whether we can hire out we will let you know. Let's hope the council sees sense and we can open our doors again in 2023".

'Walton on the Naze Beach Huts' website advises:

> "We are awaiting Tendring Council's decision on whether beach hut hire will be permitted this season and are not currently accepting bookings for 2023. We hope to release our booking calendars in early March".

Many of the smaller companies stay open over the winter and are taking bookings for 2023. One owner speaks anonymously and says:

> "It is hard to talk about it. It doesn't make sense and I am really upset about it. It was orchestrated in a diabolical manner. We think the end result will be that if we want to rent, we will have a commercial licence, but it is still not clear. I don't know why they can't come up with a clear view and cause less stress for everybody.
>
> To be quite honest there are quite a few tumble-down ones and I think they should be focusing on those ones which look derelict and are an eyesore, a target for vandalism and are a fire hazard".

RISK AND REWARD

There is money to be earned from renting beach huts, but the market is highly seasonal and appears to be less profitable than the press stories suggest. My conversations with people who own rental huts indicate that they can earn a good income in the school holidays and a bit of money in the spring and autumn. I learn that the cost of buying huts has increased but the rental prices have remained fairly stable. The market is very competitive now that there are many more available for rent. People make a profit but this is supported by hard graft — constant decorating, maintaining and cleaning. The beach hut business is run by enthusiasts, most of whom are women who enjoy the experience of spending a day at the hut themselves. The business conditions for beach hut rentals are not ideal, and continued uncertainty around the emerging beach hut strategy highlights the risk. I am reminded that despite the charm and appeal of beach huts... at the end of the day they are essentially small wooden sheds, most of which are located on Council owned land and have no security of tenure.

A hut in crisis, Eastcliff

12 — WEATHERING

Conversations about beach huts usually start with stories about best times, sunny days, birthday parties and family gatherings. Nostalgic, happy, enjoyable and memorable days. Once the pleasures of the beach hut are exhausted, some of the more mundane aspects come to the fore including the speed at which huts deteriorate. Beach huts need regular attention. Their sea front location means that they are battered by storms, dampened by sea spray and dried by the salt and sun. Paint cracks, wood rots and their wooden supports shift. I discover that huts are a work-in-progress, needing to be constantly tended, refurbished, improved and if they become too ramshackle, to be replaced.

Most commonly people tell me that they regularly paint or stain their huts and share recommendations about the best paints and techniques with their beach hut neighbours.

The majority use the pastel colour palette recommended by the Council, but in the past two years more huts have been painted with vivid colours or embellished with murals. Melanie tells me *Dalraida* has always been painted and is one of the oldest huts on Southcliff:

> "I spend a lot of time painting it... I have probably painted all around it three times in the past 13 years but the front needs more. We get waves hitting the front — even in row B and so it gets a bit damp and a bit salty. It is all original wood apart from the doors. It's made from really thick cedar boards and I wouldn't be able to replace the wood like for like, and so I have filled it a lot at the front. It is mainly filler now!"

Lynette is one of a group of owners who enjoy refurbishing huts. She previously owned *Dalraida* which required structural work when she first bought it:

> "They were going to take it down because the bearers underneath had gone at the back. I found a great guy who is a retired engineer and he loves doing jobs like that. He came with his skinny son-in-law and they jacked it all up and then the son-in-law managed to squeeze down the side and put these new bearers underneath. We saved it".

Some people have undertaken large-scale refurbishment work themselves. Frank really enjoys maintaining his hut on The Leas. Over the past 44 years he has regularly repaired the hut and has replaced much of its exterior:

> "I have replaced the wood on the outside because when we bought it, the water had started to seep in under the gloss paint and the wood was beginning to rot. We hadn't got any money really so we did it bit by bit. The first year, we did the side and the next year we did the back and then the next year the other side. And in four years we replaced all the outside. Then we made the window and changed the way it opened. The only thing that hasn't been replaced is the roof and the floor. I did it all myself".

Richard built his hut in the garden at home and then reassembled it on the beach front:

> "The hut we had was falling apart so I built this in my back garden and brought it down. I just made the whole thing including the storage for the beach toys and I bought some kitchen units and put those in. I like to make things and when I was a boy, we used to make all our own things".

The maintenance of a beach hut is on-going, but is usually identified as a pleasure. It is the active hands-on, purposeful part of having a hut and is part of the process of anticipating and planning for enjoyable days in the summer. People replace doors, mend steps, replace roof-felt, add on verandas, put in kitchens and reconfigure layouts as part of the regular process of maintaining and updating their huts. Some people enjoy painting and repairing their huts alone as it provides time for quiet contemplation and an opportunity to switch off from day-to-day life. Others talk about hut upkeep as a social activity and an opportunity to get together. I learn that a beach hut maintenance day can be an event in itself. Helen and Anne talk about the whole family coming down each year for a repairs and painting day at *Woodbairns* which involves them all working and enjoying time together by the beach.

Helen and Anne's hut is refurbished lightly with its interior unchanged because of the recollections it evokes of their parents. I discover that memories can create challenges for many owners as they try to make decisions about how to repair or replace their huts. Susan talks about the feelings aroused by her old hut *Bimbo* and the difficulties in making the decision to replace the hut built by her grandfather. Anna tells me about the challenges in maintaining the family hut on Mersea Island because any work must respect the memories of her grandmother and several great aunts. While each member of the family has access and contributes towards the maintenance the hut has become a memorial:

> "It hasn't been updated for about 30 years. It is quite retro and needs some renovation work. The problem we now face is that nobody is really sure what is going to happen to the hut. We don't know whether we will

be keeping it in the family. If we did, we could say, let's put some money in to the pot and we will all help to renovate it. Because it needs it, but over the years no one wanted to touch it in case they upset my one remaining great aunt. And also, I think there are so many sentimental parts to that hut that I don't know or understand. So, we can't take anything out or replace them because everything means something to my great aunt and she wants to keep things as they are".

While Anna has access to this hut, she prefers to spend time at *Pearl,* the hut that she owns with her husband Glenn. At *Pearl* decision making is straightforward and they love being able to renovate the hut to their own taste.

Some people like to maintain their huts themselves, others prefer to employ one of the local hut repair companies. Terry is not interested in DIY and employed someone to completely refurbish his hut just after he purchased it:

"The downside of our location at the end of The Leas is that that we get all the weather. When we bought the hut, the timbers had gone and there were gaps between the boards. And each time you went into it you would think you were in the desert because of all the sand that had accumulated inside. And all sorts of other nasties — cobwebs and all that.

I had it refurbished by a local man and it took months. He had five or six on the go and I just underestimated the work required. We have four new walls, a new roof and a new floor. This isn't a complete new build, because the frame is the same and a couple of those floor boards were there before. It was a big job and we are very pleased with it. It's nice to have the timber all sealed and painted. And we had a new kitchen and new worktops".

I also meet people who choose to replace their hut when the old one decays. They normally get one of the local companies to do this. Sue says she replaces her hut:

"about every ten years because they are wooden huts and they rot. I think this might be the third generation of hut".

When replacing a family hut the design is usually unchanged. Interiors are recreated, with bench seats, kitchens, pictures and mementos in the same place. The new hut is designed to feel just like the old one.

STORMS AND VANDALISM

The coast is regularly battered by storms and people talk about their huts being damaged during gales or swept away by floods. Ruth and Richard have had huts since the 1950s and recollect major flooding and damage caused by the North Sea floods of 1953. This storm had devastating effects on the East coast and in The Netherlands and is recollected by many beach hut owners who did not directly experience it. It is 70 years since this storm but it remains in our collective consciousness and is commemorated on its anniversaries with news stories in the press (for example Guardian, 2013; Daily Gazette 2021). We are reminded of the death toll in Essex where 104 people died, including 43 in the local area (with Jaywick and Harwich worst effected).

The most recent storm surges in 2013 and 2017 have damaged huts on Eastcliff. Emma's family previously owned two huts there and both have been damaged by storms:

> "In the 1980s there was a massive storm that wiped a
> lot of them out. We have got photographs of that. And
> since then, we have seen them being washed out to sea
> a couple of times on that stretch. Some were washed
> away about seven years ago. Our one didn't but a lot
> did. The one that my grandparents had originally
> washed away and I felt quite upset about that. Ours
> had storm doors to protect it over the winter and I
> think they prevented it from washing away completely.
> But our hut was lifted up off its supports and turned
> around a little bit. The insurance company said it was
> cheaper to replace the hut than to take it off the
> supports, repair them and put it back on again".

Lynette's huts are on the elevated section of Eastcliff:

> "The last big one we had took about seven huts out to
> sea. The sea looked as calm as a millpond. It was
> bizarre. It looked oily — it was as flat as flat. There

were no little waves like there are now, it just looked
oily. And as I got down to the bottom of the steps
suddenly the sea came up and water came rolling
down the promenade. I took a few steps back up the
slope and watched as the water came right up to the
beach huts. It was extraordinary. The water came in
at the end of the promenade and it ran down here and
the wall contained it and so it was quite powerful. It
took a lot of the hut steps off. My steps came off and
a lot of sand was deposited inside".

The most dramatic stories about storm damage are at
Eastcliff, but all along the beach, people tell me about the
additional measures that they take to protect their huts
from storms. Sue, whose hut is located up the slope on The
Leas, explains:

> "We have had a few big storms that have damaged our
> hut and we have these wires now over the roof to hold
> it in place".

Fred's hut is located on the front row at the corner on
Southcliff where:

> "There is a lot to do because the waves really hit the
> corner. We get a lot of sea-spray and we have put in
> storm doors to keep out the worst of it".

Helen and Anne's hut is on the corner of High Wall and The
Leas:

"We have had storm boards put on the front and they fold back. We are on the end of a row and can really get the weather. We always lock the storm doors when we leave. Even in the summer. One of them got ripped off in the storm a couple of weeks ago. Some friends were here for the day and when they arrived, they folded the doors back and hooked them up. It was a lovely hot day and they went for a walk and just locked up the main hut door. While they were away the storm came in and it was so vicious that it ripped off the storm door and sent it down the promenade. They said that they couldn't believe it because when they came back and the door was right down at the other end of the path".

While people accept that storm damage is part of the experience of owning a hut, many express frustration and annoyance about vandalism. Most commonly people tell me about their steps being smashed or doors being kicked open. I hear that there is more vandalism in the back row huts because they are tucked away and not overlooked by passing walkers. Many rental huts have key boxes fitted and I hear that that these are regularly knocked off. Several tell me that people have broken into their huts to sleep in them over the winter. No one I speak to leaves anything valuable in their hut in the winter and no one reports having had belongings stolen from their own hut. Sue talks about the huts on The Leas:

"There is a lot of vandalism. Security is a big thing. People have tried to kick in my beach hut door a couple of times. When we had the old beach hut someone did break into it and lived in it for a while. When we came in the spring, there were empty tins and a sleeping bag had been discarded. They didn't break anything. It was just homeless people and I didn't mind that. It is different when its mindless vandalism".

Phillip and Maureen's hut is located mid row on High Wall in Frinton:

"We don't worry about the weather that much but it's vandals. People have put in double doors — less for the storm and more for security. A few have been burnt near here and next-door people broke in and threw paint around. It was that black tar paint that you put on the roof. They threw it all around and made a real mess and someone kicked in all the steps the year we moved in".

Carol's hut is on High Wall:

"In my last hut we were broken into. It was just malicious damage, it was knocked about but nothing was taken. The door was broken and they damaged the inside. Just for a bit of fun! Now I have a thick bar across my doors to stop people from kicking them in".

Mary is on Low Wall and tells me that one evening a group

of people were running and jumping along the roofs of the huts which caused structural damage to her roof. Lynette also talks about the problem of people running along the roofs:

> "A lot of the new huts are designed with steep roof pitches because if the roofs are too flat then the kids run on them".

Fires are also identified as a major risk as most huts contain gas canisters to supply cookers and many people use candles for lighting in the evening. These tightly packed wooden boxes are highly flammable but very few have fire extinguishers or fire-blankets. There are no firebreak walls, limited water supplies and it is difficult for emergency services to access the promenade. Once started beach hut fires can spread fast and are hard to control.

Some people attribute beach hut fires to bored local youth looking for some excitement. Lynette says that it is not unusual for the fires to be started intentionally and tells me that when she was on Southcliff:

> "There were about four or five huts burned down and my lovely hut was the last one. The side was burned but it was saveable. We had to replace the side... but it didn't get inside because it was double skinned".

However, most people I speak to say that beach hut fires start as the result of accidents. I hear that there is a bigger fire danger in some of the rental huts because renters are unfamiliar with the vagaries of the gas stove. Many struggle with connecting the canisters and don't really understand the conventions and safety procedures associated with the makeshift cooking arrangements in the hut. In 2022 one of the rental huts in Walton has its aging gas stove disconnected by beach hut association members after people in neighbouring huts complain about the smell of gas.

In August 2019 a large fire sweeps along the huts at Low Wall in Frinton, destroying 12 in one afternoon. Steph tells me that this fire was caused by a leaky gas canister and that it spread quickly due to strong winds. I am further down the beach that day but I hear the fire-engines and see the smoke. The next morning, I walk along to see the blackened skeletal remains of these huts. They are surrounded by police tape and one has charred possessions still inside.

ANATOMY OF A DEAD HUT

Charred wood
A bench
A windbreak
A bucket
A metal table
A storage bench
A melted swimming float
A blackened hob
Some dirty rags
Police tape.

Storm surge, Eastcliff

AT THE END OF SUMMER

The days are getting cooler, it has been stormy in the night, but this morning the rain has stopped. I spend a day walking along the promenade to update my hut survey. I normally walk along the beach and from this distance the huts are pastel perfection but as I stroll slowly along the promenade there is a sense of desolation. The toilets and cafes are shut. I hike up the steep steps and along the narrow paths on Southcliff, it feels simultaneously like an enchanted village and a shantytown. Many huts are shuttered up for the winter, paint is peeling, bolts are rusting and wood is rotting. I watch as a rat ambles back home to its warm nest under one of the huts, and remind myself that a hut is a responsibility as well as a pleasure.

Relaxed, Southcliff

13 — FEELINGS

A beach hut provides shelter and is a base for coastal visits through the seasons. It is a place to pause, to notice, to enjoy the natural environment and to reflect. Regular visits create familiarity and can evoke an understanding of the rhythms of the sea. Beach hut people become aware of the sea's currents, notice neap and spring tides, and discern subtle changes to the beach as it is revealed by the ebbing tide each day. Many of the people I meet at their huts share a respect for the power of the sea and love of the unpredictable nature of coastal weather. This way of knowing and being creates a beach identity, supported by beach hut rituals and practices that follow the rhythms of tide and weather.

Sense of alignment with the environment and disconnection from the stresses and worries of everyday life cues a way of feeling; and an emotional and embodied attachment to hut and beach. When I ask people how a day at the hut makes them feel they pause and smile, but often find it difficult to express these feelings. Many make short responses using words like relaxed, calm or happy. At the beach hut they are occupied but not busy; simultaneously in nature and at a place that feels homely and familiar. The sense of having enough and being enough is profound, but it is often difficult to find words to express these feelings and emotions.

HAPPY

Amy, Sue, Steph and Anna all identify the beach hut as their "happy place". Sue explains her use of the phrase:

> "I remember listening to Claire Baldwin on *Ramblings* (Radio Programme) and she was talking to somebody about a fantastic view and it was the view from his home. And then they were talking about the way that your memories affect your perception of a place or a view. Claire Baldwin said her happy place is the Cotswolds because that is where her memories are from. And so, this is my happy place. I look out here, and to me this is idyllic. I love this view. I love being here. It makes me feel very relaxed and very happy, and it brings back memories of childhood".

Anna's "happy place" arises from a combination of the environment and being away from day-to-day chores:

"Even when you have the waves crashing on the shore and you are just sitting in here it is so relaxing. And yeah I can potter about here. but I can't do the washing, or the ironing and I can't do the gardening. I just have to make sure that the kids are happy and I really enjoy it. And with the hustle and bustle of daily life you need that! Especially in lockdown which was nuts. I was home-schooling Pippa and I was still in work. My husband was working from home and I was trying to keep everybody happy. It was bonkers! So, coming down here was a breath of fresh air... and we needed that. But it is my happy space. And at home there is always something to be done. And here — not so much. I can stop and I take note of everything around and I love to watch happy people. Everyone is just so happy and friendly here. It is a different pace of life and you need that".

Like Anna many of the women I speak to identify the hut as a place where they can get away from day-to-day chores and responsibilities. Even Nina who rents three huts and spends much of her time working hard to clean, maintain and style her huts perceives that the hut is a place where she can disconnected from chores and worries:

"I don't want to go home when I am here. I just want to stay. It is like you are in a bubble or on the edge. All your responsibilities are somewhere else. Everyone is friendly and it is lovely and welcoming".

Anne also feels disconnected from all of the worries and stresses of daily life when she is at her hut:

> "It is just like being in a different world. Even when it is busy down here it doesn't feel busy. I just have a feeling of total relaxation and happiness".

For Steph the beach hut is her:

> "... happy place because I feel peaceful, calm and tranquil. It's familiar! It's like putting on a comfy jumper or a pair of slippers, I think. I know the place, know the water, know the beach and what is going to happen. And it is just relaxing and there is nothing unexpected. It is just comfortable".

RELAXED

Emma is one of the many people who make short responses when I ask about her feelings at the beach hut. She identifies a sense of:

> "total relaxation. You just feel calm here".

Several other people initially make a one-word response 'relaxed' but then after a pause start to explain what it is about the beach hut that makes them feel relaxed. For Helen:

> "It feels like a release... because you have escaped from everything that is going on. It is just an escape, it really is".

The beach setting makes Sarah feel relaxed:

> "I feel really relaxed. Everything that I worry about just
> goes. I think it is the space and the blue of the sea and
> sky. It brings me down to earth and I get here and
> think 'why am I so stressed about this and that?' Being
> here gives me hope. I love seeing the little children
> sitting and playing on the beach, and breathing sea air
> and all those things".

Karen also talks about the effect of being close to the sea:

> "I feel calm and rejuvenated. There is something about
> the sea air. They say it is good for you and I think that
> it is. It is lovely. Even if I have been here just for the day,
> I feel like I have been here for a week!"

TIRED

Many people say a day at the beach hut makes them feel
tired. In another context tiredness might have a negative
connotation, be associated with stress, doing too much and
with being overwhelmed. However in the beach hut setting,
tiredness is always presented in a positive way. Richard
attributes his beach hut tiredness to the fresh air:

> "At the end of the day you go home really tired. It is a
> long-lasting feeling. It's a good tired and I love it.
> I love the water. I love the beach. I don't know how
> I would sum up the whole feeling but you always go

home really tired. It's the fresh-air, I think. And you sleep well after a day at the hut".

Sue thinks her beach hut tiredness might have something to do with the sea and feeling calm:

"As you go home you don't stop yawning. It's a combination of being by the sea and being so peaceful. Every day is a pleasant memory in itself and often it is nothing special. But you go home tired and it's just nice".

Sophie also associates beach hut tiredness with being at the coast and feeling relaxed:

"We always sleep so much better and it is a combination of the sea, the sea air and just being so chilled. Generally, we rush about, and here we can just take things slower. I can go in the water and then come back up to the hut and relax".

Helen talks about the Alfie and Annie Rose books by Shirley Hughes. She used to read them to her children and remembers a story from *Alfie: The Big Alfie Out of Doors Storybook* in which the children visit the beach. She makes parallels between the story and her own feelings about spending a day at the beach hut:

"It is a lovely illustrated book about the beach and when I see those pictures it captures how I feel.

I share Annie Rose's wonder, when she finds the stone and can understand her being upset when she has to go home. I love just being here and then going home tired and sandy at the end of the day. When the children were young, we would try to wash all the sand and the salt off them before we went home. And then they would run into the sea again. I love the way the salt and the sand stay with you and so you still have that feeling of the beach when you get home".

REFLECTIONS ON THE ENVIRONMENT

One of the pleasures of having a hut is that it provides a base for regular visits throughout the year. Hut owners are able to experience the variety of conditions at the beach in different seasons. Sue loves visiting her hut in the winter:

"Sometimes when we come down in the winter and it is windy, the sand is just rolling across the beach. It is quite phenomenal, like a sandstorm and all the breakwaters seem to disappear. We just sit here and watch. Sometimes we watch the sand blowing, other times we come here during a storm and watch the thunder and lightning. One day when you come after a storm the beach might be full of pebbles and then the next time it is just sand. It can change so much, especially in the winter".

Graham visits throughout the year:

"It is so relaxing being by water. I really enjoy being by the sea. I love it in all conditions and especially when it is stormy".

Debbie and her husband have a hut on the corner of The Leas and Southcliff. A combination of the curve in the coastline and the sea defences mean that this is the place to witness the largest waves on this stretch of beach. Watching the power of the sea is one of the many pleasures afforded by their beach hut and at high tide they love to watch as waves explode onto the promenade:

"We come in all weathers. We visit when we have thunderstorms and those stormy days when the waves come crashing over the wall. We just sit and watch as people walk around the corner and get soaked by the next big wave. Some stand there with their phones and iPads ready to take photos of the waves, and the next moment they are soaked".

Phillip loves to visit his hut in the winter:

"I like to see all the elements. We come here in the winter when it is really windy and we love to watch a storm coming in. We have a plastic window and we can sit in the dry and watch the purple clouds, the dark lines of rain showers across the sea, and the rain getting stronger and stronger. The beauty of being right on the coast, is that we get a panoramic view".

When I first meet Robert and Lindsey they have only just bought a hut but after our first meeting I see them regularly when I walk along the beach. They have become out-of-season regulars and Robert swims throughout the year:

> "We like coming here when it is stormy for the noise, the colour, the crashing of the waves and the shapes of the clouds. We like it in all weathers really and it is lovely to be able to see the horizon. Here you get that sense of space".

Mary has strong faith and tells me that her beach hut is a place where she can appreciate the natural environment and feel a real spiritual connection as well. She loves to visit on her own, to sit gazing at the sea and to reflect upon her faith:

> "People underestimate the sea's power and it makes me think about God's power which has unknown limits. When I look at the sea, I feel awe. I feel small in the face of the powerful forces of nature".

She talks about the rhythms of the sea, the regularity of its ebbs and flows. She loves the juxtaposition of aspects that are dependable and inevitable, that "will never let you down" and those things that are different each time she visits. Sometimes the sea is all "stillness, calmness, serenity and peace" on others it is "noisy, stormy and rough". She reflects on the tides and the way the beach is covered and completely washed clean at high tide:

"As the tide goes out you are left with perfection... until you walk on it. It makes me think about the way Christ comes into your life and wipes it clean".

Jemima's hut is her place for reflection. However her cues are environmental rather than spiritual:

"I describe it to people as my sanctuary because it is just my place. You arrive with your worries and woes, all the stuff that is going on in your life. You are busy at work, you have stuff on your mind and responsibilities. And you just come here and listen to the water, sit here in the fresh air and it feels amazing. If you are in a bad mood — it's gone".

For Emma the sound and sight of the sea enables contemplation:

"If I am worried about something that is my go-to place. I can go there and just think — just have time to myself away from everything and everybody. If I need to think, I like to be by the sea. When people in my family have died, my first instinct is to go to the beach and have time by myself. It is a place where I can lose myself, watch the waves, watch the water and I could be anywhere".

Fred tells me that the Coronavirus Pandemic has made him feel low but that a day at the hut lifts his spirits and makes him feel happier.

"Just lately during lockdown I have got a bit down. A bit fed up. And now I can come down here and it is just incredible. It changes your mood. You can look at the sea all day long really. I am hoping that it will be easier this summer with more people vaccinated and I am looking forward to spending more time here".

THE HUT AS A SANCTUARY

The idea of the hut as a sanctuary is held by many beach hutters, and reflected in names such as *Seaside Sanctuary, Resthaven* and *Haven*. Sarah shared her hut with a friend when she was unwell:

"Three years ago, she was diagnosed with quite a serious illness. She had all her chemo and was really sick. And that summer we came here about four times a week. She just didn't want to go out anywhere with people but she would come down here. And I just remember how nice it was, what a good feeling it gave me just to spend time with her and share this space".

Lynette also invites friends who are sick or convalescing:

"I have had a couple of friends who haven't been very well and they have just got enough energy or life left to make it down here. Not too long ago someone came and she had never been to a beach hut before. She wasn't here long, came for a simple lunch and just gazed out. I felt good about doing it. It gave me a nice feeling".

The wellbeing effects of the huts are felt by both women's guests and by the women themselves, because they have positive feelings associated with being kind and supporting their friends. Several people talk about visiting with elderly parents. Emma recalls her mother visiting the hut when she was sick:

> "For the last eight years of her life mum had been unwell and it was quite difficult for her to get to the beach. So, when we got her to the hut it was a really special occasion. Sometimes she came in a wheelchair, other times she could walk really slowly. And two years ago, was the last time she came down. We were having a party for my son. My mum said 'I don't think I can come'. But we managed to get her down here in a wheelchair. She said that she would only stay for ten minutes but in the end, she stayed for about four hours. And she just loved sitting watching all of the grandchildren together, and being on the beach, and looking the sea. And there was no pressure at the hut she didn't have to do anything. Being here with her made me feel so good".

Other stories about people's emotions and feelings have been shared in the *MEMORIES* chapter. It is clear that many hut owners have a particular emotional attachment to their hut because it is an important part of their history together as a family.

KNOWING AND BEING

Regularly visiting a beach hut supports familiarity with the sea, a sense of the tides, of the direction of the undertow, of the waves, and the wildlife. This specific way of knowing and being at the beach is learned and stems from multiple visits across the seasons. It is shaped by childhood experiences, family traditions, and by an accumulation of memories, encounters and interactions. The hut provides a little bit of home on the coast and has various functions. It is a play-house, a safe place to shelter from the rain, a changing place, a storage box and a repository for memories. It enables a privileged encounter with the beach, and sustained engagement creates a deep and nuanced understanding. Steph contrast the behaviour of beach hutters and day trippers:

> "I don't think day trippers understand the ethos and integrity of the beach. At the end of the day they don't care what they leave behind. And I think 'you have had a nice day — don't just walk away from your mess!' What I don't like now is the disposable barbecues. In the past there wasn't such a thing. And now you get people lighting barbecues on the beach which means other people can't play football and it is a fire hazard. They don't consider other people on the beach. I feel like I want to write 'no barbecues' in the sand".

Many tell me that picking up the rubbish that others leave on the beach is a standard part of their beach hut day.

Emma says during the summers of 2020 and 2021 the beaches have been more crowded and people seem to leave more rubbish behind:

> "We clear up the beaches in the evening. We take a bag with us and pick up rubbish. We have never bought any buckets and spades ever because so much stuff is left at the end of the day by other people. We are not dog owners but the beach here is dog-friendly and we bring plastic bags down here so if someone's dog makes a mess and tries to walk away, we give them a bag. It takes a lot of guts to do that but you don't want your children standing in it".

Sue comments:

> "The people who come for day trips are more likely to drop litter because they do not have that sense of ownership".

Several people say that many day trippers don't understand the tides and currents. Carol often watches families setting up elaborate camps just in front of the incoming tide:

> "The other week these people set up. They put out all their chairs and their windbreaks and their tables, and then the tide started to come in and so they moved back a little bit. Then by the time they had set up again it had come in some more and so they moved back a bit. In the end I think that they moved about six times...

and then they came up onto the steps but it was a very high tide and it came up there as well. Sometimes it is funny to watch people when they just don't understand the tide".

Steph tells about the currents around the pier at Walton and at nearby Clacton and the occasional drownings on nearby beaches:

"We do have strong currents here, but it is really shallow and so if you stay in your depth it's really safe. A couple of years ago several children drowned in Clacton. They were day trippers from Luton and they were not aware of the water or the tides. They were not strong swimmers and they went out of their depth too close to the pier and got sucked in to the currents around it".

This incident in 2019 is covered in the press (BBC, 2020), and since then there have been several more near drownings and another death in 2022 (BBC, 2022).

Emma recalls a particular incident where a small child on an inflatable was swept out to sea:

"We have seen a lot of things blow out to sea. Once my ex-husband rescued a three year-old who was floating on a bodyboard. We were swimming just out of our depth and this child floated out past us on a bodyboard. It was really scary. The parents were sat chatting outside the beach hut that they had hired and they hadn't noticed. When we bought him back in and explained what had happened and about the strong off-shore wind they didn't seem to be bothered. It shocked us!"

Susan tells me that in her hut:

"We have four huge rubber rings and there is always a long length of blue bailer twine, because on any coast you have got to know what the conditions are. When we were little we saw enough balls, lilos and rubber rings float out to sea. And sadly I remember the vicar from Thorpe's son drowning on our beach when I was a child. My dad made sure that we were always been very aware of safety. We still have the blue rope and we all joke about it".

I hear many stories about day trippers having little understanding of the vagaries of the coast. About the people who arrive at high tide and are shocked that the beach has disappeared. People who arrive laden with beach towels, buckets and spades in large bags or pull along trollies, but are ill-prepared for unpredictable seaside weather. Some days they can be seen shivering and goose-pimpled as cold sea-mists sit thick and heavy on the beach but are completely absent 100 meters inland. On clear days they sit in the strong sun which is masked by the cool sea breeze and their skin reddens. On windy days they sit huddled on the beach eating sandwiches dusted with a gritty coating of sand. Rain showers chase day trippers into the town cafes to seek shelter, or back to the station to board the next train home. In contrast hut owners can shelter inside, put on extra layers, drink tea, eat cake and play cards until the rain has passed or the wind has died down.

Time at the hut creates a particular relationship with the beach. Repeated visits lead to familiarity and understanding. Owning a beach hut provides shelter and motivation to visit the beach regularly, at different times of the day, throughout the year, and in different weather conditions. Beach hut owners can enjoy watching storms from the shelter of their hut, pop down for a cup of tea, have a brief escape from mundane chores or spend long days at the beach. The beach hut offers a base, privacy and sense of security in knowing what you will find within your small space of self-created paradise. Anne says:

> "Well you know everything changes Everything changes apart from Frinton beach. There is something about a day at the hut that is unchanging. It is lovely partly because you know what to expect and then it is just what you expected it to be".

Beach walk, Walton

14 — BECOMING

As I collect stories for this book I begin to understand the appeal of a beach hut. I encounter some people who are energetic and restless. For them the beach hut is a project, the base for active play around a busy day of cooking, swimming, walking, sandcastles and socialising. Other people engage in quieter leisure pursuits at their huts and spend their days chatting, reading, knitting, and painting. A few like to visit alone to sit and contemplate the sea, daydream, sunbathe and sleep.

Beach hut people enjoy spending time away from the mundane domesticity of home and garden. Many of the women tell me that home is a place where there are never-ending chores and things to do. The beach hut is a Wendy house, playful and back-to-basics. It is small-scale, manageable, a space where women can really relax.

Melanie explains:

> "I feel I am in control here. At home there is so much to
> do and things are probably looking a little scruffy
> whereas here I am on top of things all the time. This
> the only space that is really mine and I keep it painted
> nicely, and I am tidy, and I clean it. This is my space".

I am a slow learner but I am beginning to understand. I know
my way around a beach hut, have a better understanding of
the people that choose to spend time in them. I feel an
affinity with the welcoming and friendly community of
beach hutters' at Frinton and Walton. As I have collected
information for this book I have spoken to strangers, asked
them questions and found out more about their lives. I have
been invited to join people and to listen to the stories,
memories, and feelings that are evoked by a day at the hut.

In the summer of 2022, I meet Eleanor and discover
someone else who is on a beach hut journey — one that is
completely different to my own. Eleanor's first beach hut
experience was on her 31st birthday:

> "A friend had been given a free beach hut day and so
> we came for my birthday. I hadn't been to Walton
> before and I remember arriving, and walking down a
> small grass path, and it felt exciting. The owner took
> us there and opened the door and it was fun to unpack
> it. My friend brought a cake and we brought food to
> eat for lunch.

I remember going for a swim at high tide. It was September, the sea was warm. Then after the swim we walked along the narrow uneven paths trying to find our way back to the hut. It felt so weird and wonky. Such as secret space".

After that first experience, she continues to hire huts for special occasions. She moves to Walton and opens The Nose bookshop. At the start of 2022 Eleanor makes a New Year's resolution to hire a different hut every month:

"It was a way of being social — of inviting my friends to come and visit me. I thought it was something that people might like to come to. That I would get some drinks and make some lunch, and different people might come each time. It would be a place where different groups of friends could hang out with each other.

I called it 'Beach Hut Club' and I invited people to join and come along. The plan was that I would send an email to share the location and tell them what was going to happen. I wanted to book one each month in different locations. I started in January, there were about 6 of us and we went to *Seahorse* on Southcliff. It was really nice day. We had lunch, sat on the steps, went swimming and got cold. It was fun! "

Eleanor and I both want to know more about beach huts but take very different paths. At the start of my journey I don't really like beach huts and I am trying to understand why other people do. I am a voyeur I spend time at huts talking to beach hutters' but am a visitor and an outsider. Several neighbours offer to lend me their huts. I don't take up their offers. I like beach hut people but am not convinced about the huts themselves. I really don't want to spend a day confined within one.

In contrast Eleanor enjoys beach huts and immerses herself in a variety of different beach hut experiences with her friends, learning more from each one. She quickly becomes a beach hut person and acquires an understanding of the advantages and opportunities at different locations along the beach that I don't have. She knows about the seasonal variations along this stretch of coast and the closure of toilets and standpipes in some locations in the Autumn:

> "In February I rented one on the Walings as I wanted a deck with the afternoon sun. Just a few people came, but it was a sunny day and we went on a windswept walk up to Holland-on-Sea. The loo wasn't open and the taps were turned off so you couldn't get any water".

Some months she rents huts which are tucked away up the slope and others amongst the crowds on the prom near the pier:

> "The summer ones were fun and now I appreciate being on the front row. I never would have thought it

was a good place to be, but there is something about putting the chairs out on the front and being part of the hubbub. The August Bank Holiday was one of my favourite ones. We were in Nina's hut *Dragonfly*, which is such as party hut. It is colourful, kitsch, feels like a hen-do hut, the sort of place where you are meant to put your sun-glasses on, drink prosecco, get a bit pissed, take some pictures, and put them on Instagram".

I tell her about the book and send her a few chapters. We talk more about our projects and in September she invites me to join her and a group of friends at a hut on The Leas. She warns:

> "I've got a funny feeling it might be the one you
> describe as the cold, windy, miserable one. The one
> that you visited with your friend at the start of your
> beach hut journey".

I imagine how the hut might have changed in the 17 or 18 years since I last visited. I think of the beautifully designed interiors of the hire huts on Southcliff and Eastcliff and picture a pastel hut decked out in Cath Kidson fabrics and adorned with bunting.

When we arrive, the hut has already been opened and seats placed outside. People are milling around and the sun has just come out. I climb up the steps and peer inside into a time-warp. Dark timber walls, a tiny old-fashioned kitchen, an old table and an aging bench seat. Instead of bunting this hut is festooned with instructions. Passive aggressive directions are pasted everywhere and supplemented by a booklet with photos so that the renter can leave things exactly as they found them. The hut is clean, but feels bleak and unwelcoming. I don't like this hut at all, but now I understand why. The design doesn't capture a sense of play, or pleasure and the messages dispel any notion of welcome, warmth and friendliness.

The day with Eleanor and her friends is so much more than the unfriendly hut. I love the experience of sitting outside on the grassy slope in the sunshine. I have no responsibilities. There are children here but they are not mine. I don't have to worry when they disappear out of sight or get bored. I can meet new people, swim, chat, laugh, eat paella and tortilla, drink wine and chat some more. Eleanor is relaxed, a great host, and invites me to join her again.

October's hut is set back in row C on Southcliff. It is cool and windy, and there are just the two of us at the hut. We look around the interior. It is blue and white with three beach themed pictures on one side, a bench seat with storage underneath, a boat shape framed mirror, a blue kitchen and blue cups and crockery. Eleanor makes tea and we eat cake as we watch the sea. She tells me about her experiences of visiting different huts each month with various friends:

"Often when I am with a group of people, we don't
spend any time in the hut. When I am on my own, or
with one or two people we sit inside and have a chat
and cook in the hut. But when there is a larger group,
we are on the veranda or if people have kids they are
always running to the beach. It is funny that
sometimes you think you are coming to the hut but
you hardly spend any time in there".

This hut is clean and comfortable. There is a guest book
and we look through the messages and drawings from
previous renters who share their experiences of a perfect
day at the hut. We don't spend any time on the beach but
look out over the sea while we chat. At the end of the
afternoon I feel calm and relaxed.

I decide that it is time to spend some time in beach huts
on my own as I finish this book. At the end of October Clive
lends me his hut on the Walings. It is a chilly afternoon and
there are few people on the beach. I shut the hut door to cut
myself off from walkers on the sea wall and open one of the
large windows that look out over the sea. The hut has a
built-in white kitchen with brightly coloured glasses and
plates on open shelves. There is a paddleboard on one side,
a homemade bird-kite with 'Father Clive' written across its
back, and bunting hangs from the wall. I clear a space at the
table and prepare for an afternoon of writing. It takes a
while to settle. This is an unfamiliar space, and initially the
view out toward the horizon is a distraction. As I watch

I feel each breath lengthening, my shoulders loosen, my inner voice quietens... my thoughts drift

The sea is gloomy, gently undulating, dappled grey and I watch as flecks of light catch its ripples. The clouds cast deep shadows, darkening much of its surface. In a few spots weak sunlight breaks through and here its greyness pales and is tinged with blue. Near the horizon it appears flat, closer to the shore I can see its turbulence as water gathers into peaks and is hurled landward. The waves break, white in the places where countless droplets refract the light. By the hut the sea looks dull brown and is thick with sand. I listen to the whisper of the waves as I watch them ebb and flow. I reach for my thermos, pour myself a cup of tea, sip and watch. I suspect that I won't write. At first this worries me because I came here to write. My perspective shifts, this is a special moment, the writing doesn't matter. I sit, watch and listen to the tide coming in. The rhythmic resonance of the waves becomes everything. I relax, follow my drifting thoughts, feel calm and then I start to write. I lose time and write until the sky is darkening and my fingers are numb with the cold.

At the start of November Nina lends me *Ladybird* one of her rental huts on Southcliff. I have been inside this hut before and know that it is beautifully styled and packed full of ornaments and books. It is a stormy day and as I walk down the slope the whole beach is in motion, a haze of airborne grains. The shifting sandscape seems treacherous, I leap off the bottom step and launch myself into its flow. I let go as the wind propels me. Raising my arms as I drift, glide and soar, become a human kite. Shoved by a gust I lurch, stumble, rebalance and fly forward again. I arrive exhilarated, much to edgy to write. I unlock the storm doors and take time to explore the interior. There is a lot to see, an array of games, pictures, brightly coloured glasses and pretty teacups. The bench seat is at the back, shelving on either side and there are ladybirds everywhere, a ladybird kettle and mugs, ladybird books, ladybird curtains, and cushions. There is a small hob and jars full of tea-bags. I fill up the kettle at the closest standpipe, connect the gas cannister and turn on the small gas hob. I have learned from my previous experience and unpack my provisions; sandwiches, cake, fresh milk and a hot water bottle. The water boils and I settle down near the window, mug of tea in hand and hot water bottle on my lap.

The beach hut provides shelter and comfort, and a ringside seat from which I can view the ongoing storm. The sky is alive, one moment blue, with white clouds racing from the south; the next it is grey and dark, its dense clouds carrying a deluge of horizontal rain. The wind gusts, howling around the hut and the sea rages. Waves crash against the sea wall, splashing sand and saltwater over the roofs of the huts by the promenade. I have a sense of being on a boat at sea. I close my eyes as I hang on tight ready for the heave, brace myself for a tilt, a roll and the wall of spray. I am surprised when there is no motion, no sea-spray. The wind rages all around, doors rattle but I am safe in the shelter of the hut. I start to write and this time write until

the storm lulls and I am hungry. I venture outside, gaze up
at the shuttered beach hut village and then out over the
beach. Sand whips along and I can see no one. I eat lunch,
drink tea, refill the hot water bottle and then write again.
Time vanishes and I write until the light is failing

Why is the hut a good place to write? I am perplexed.
I thought I needed stillness and order, and a hut offers
neither. There is so much going on outside and the interior
is chockfull of stuff. In general, I don't like clutter, find it
oppressive, but in a borrowed hut I can relax. It's not my
clutter and therefore does not need to be thought about,
sorted, or arranged. In both huts I spend time acknowledging
the things inside, note what is there and then let it go. It is
there, a backdrop and nothing more. The ever-changing
sea and sky are initially distracting but as I gaze at the
horizon I am drawn in. This view is calming and reassuring
even on a stormy day. The sound of the sea lulls me into a
contemplative state and I am ready to write.

So, as I come to the end of this book I am just beginning
to understand the appeal of a beach hut. There is a pleasing
rhythm to beach hut life which follows the seasons. In the
Autumn, a bolting down, locking of storm doors —
protection over the winter months. In winter a sort of
hibernation. Few people visit and those that do either sit
inside drinking tea or huddle outside in thick coats and
wrapped in blankets. Spring is a hopeful time, an
awakening with renewed activity as the beach hutters start
to paint and prepare for the summer ahead. Summer is the

time to relax and to entertain. There is a joy in being part of a beach hut community, feeling a sense of belonging and having an in-depth knowledge of one section of beach.

Beach huts evoke stories, recollections of childhood. Not my childhood, but a childhood that chimes with some of my own memories and is appealing. I am beginning to understand why generation after generation of beach hutters strive to create similar memories for their children.

I have learned more about beach hut stuff — the pictures, ornaments, plates, jars, collections, mugs that line beach hut shelves. I now know that that things on display in beach huts are imbued with subtle, personal meanings. I am starting to understand that this stuff is not clutter, and have reimagined it as an eclectic family archive which prompts people to journey to the past, pause, reflect and reminisce together. I find it difficult to imagine the sensory overload that I would experience if I physically entered a space from childhood and was surrounded by my grandparents things. I am envious of the beach hut people who can time travel like Dr Who in the Tardis.

In a beach hut, time has an elastic quality, simultaneously stretching-out and slipping away. Hours are lost in the busyness of doing little... a chat with friends, people watching, a paddle and the whole day is gone. And when you ask people what they do at the beach hut many say... 'well nothing really'. And finally I realised that in that nothing is everything. The beach hut is dedicated to providing its occupants with the freedom just to be.

POSTSCRIPT

I am sitting in my imagined beach hut *Ada*, looking out
over the sea. In this fantasy future life, I have learned to
embrace beach hut time and have become altogether
calmer and more reflective. I have learned how to pause
and to switch off. I am less driven, and have developed a
sense of perspective which embraces the beach environment.
My fictional beach hut houses collections of stones, and
shells, and is lined with bookshelves. All my hidden books
have been liberated. Seasoned hut owners will tell you that
the beach hut is not a good place to store books... pages
dampen and curl... but I do not have these problems in my
make-believe beach hut which is perfect for book storage.
So here I sit... sometimes I write, but mostly I just sit and
watch the sea.

REFERENCES

2 PEOPLE

Tom Bolton (2018) *Low Country: Brexit on the Essex Coast*. Penned in the Margins.

3 PLACE

Ben Eagle (2015) *Pushed to the Edge: A History of the Naze and Walton Hall*. Completely Novel.

Clacton and Frinton Gazette (2021) Frinton residents divided over the arrival of a mobile ice cream vendor. https://www.clactonandfrintongazette.co.uk/news/19534663.frinton-residents-divided-arrival-mobile-ice-cream-vendor.

Daily Mail (2020) Frinton on Sea fights 'rush' of rogue ice cream sellers. https://www.dailymail.co.uk/news/article-8611873/Affluent-seaside-town-Essex-goes-war-rush-rogue-ice-cream-sellers.html.

Michael Rouse (2013) *Frinton and Walton Through Time*. Amberley Publishing.

Norman Jacobs (1995) *Frinton and Walton: A Pictorial History*. Phillimore and Co.

Steven Walker (2020) *The Naze: Walton on the Naze*. Independently Published.

Telegraph (2021) Ice cream van whips sleepy Frinton into a frenzy. https://www.telegraph.co.uk/news/2021/08/25/ice-cream-seller-whips-sleepy-frinton-frenzy/.

Times (2021) Tourism-shy Frinton-on-Sea acts to freeze out ice cream sellers. https://www.thetimes.co.uk/article/tourism-shy-frinton-on-sea-acts-to-freeze-out-ice-cream-sellers-25zxbq6q6#:~:text=The%20tranquil%20Essex%20town%20where,selling%20treats%20on%20the%20prom.

Tendring District Council (2021) Tourism Strategy for Tendring 2021-2026. https://tdcdemocracy.tendringdc.gov.uk/documents/s33219/A8%20Appendix%20Draft%20Tourism%20Strategy%202021%202026.pdf.

4 BUYING

Brent Heavener (2019) *Tiny House: Live Small, Dream Big*. Ebury Press.

Gill Heriz (2014) *A Woman's Shed: Spaces for women to create, write, make, grow, think, and escape*. CICO Books.

Tom Bolton (2018) *Low Country: Brexit on the Essex Coast*. Penned in the Margins.

Zach Klein and Steven Lockhart (2015) *Cabin Porn*. Particular Books.

6 CRAFT

Rachel Hunt (2018) On sawing a loaf: living simply and skilfully in hut and bothy. *Cultural Geographies*. *25 (1) 71-89*.

10 STORIES

Charlotte Linde (2013) *Life Stories: The Creation of Coherence*. Oxford University Press.

Jonathan Gottschall (2012) *The Storytelling Animal: How stories make us human*. Houghton Mifflen, Harcourt.

Molbjerg Jorgensen, K. (2017). *Tell me a souvenir: storytelling-destination perspectives and tourism globalisation*, TEFI Conference — Building Our Stories. Copenhagen. August 2017.

12 WEATHERING

Daily Gazette Essex County Standard (2021) https://www.gazette-news.co.uk/news/19057589.deadly-1953-floods-devastated-essex-coast/.

Guardian (2013) https://www.theguardian.com/environment/gallery/2013/jan/31/devastation-east-anglia-1953-flood-in-pictures.

BBC (2020) Clacton sea deaths: Brother and sister died in 'tragic accident'.

https://www.bbc.co.uk/news/uk-england-essex-51532599.

BBC (2022) Clacton: Swimmer missing after five saved from sea

https://www.bbc.co.uk/news/uk-england-essex-62215895.

Shirley Hughes (1992) Alfie: *The Big Alfie Out of Doors Storybook*. Red Fox.

PICTURE CREDITS

ACKNOWLEDGEMENTS

A big thank you to all the people who shared their stories with me —
Anna and Glenn; Anne, Helen and Mavis; Carol, Dawn, Debbie,
Dierdre, Dorothy, Eleanor, Emma, Ersilia, Frank and Marion; George
and Catherine; Graham and Angela; Jemima, Jenny, Geoff and Amy;
John and Betty; June and Peter; Karen, Kevin and Sophie; Lauren,
Linda and Nick; Lindsey, Lynette and Rebecca; Margaret, Mary,
Melanie (Walton Beach Hut Association), Nina, Paul and Vicky; Phillip
and Maureen; Richard and Pam; Roger, Ruth and Clifford; Robert and
Lindsey; Rob and Laura; Sally, Sarah and Martin; Sue, Susan, Steph,
Terry and Olivia; Victoria.

Also thank you to everyone who gave me feedback on draft chapters
of this book — Lizzy Bennett, Kate Forman, Charlie Inskip, Lee Johnson,
Faye Rathe, Tina Seskis, Clare Shaw, Ken Worpole.

To Crispin Wright for drawing the map and beach hut illustrations.
To Sam Johnson Schlee and Gordon Wise for providing sound advice as
I looked for a publisher. Clive Brill and Nina Chinsky for lending me their
beach huts as I was writing the last chapter of the book.

To my inspirational writing groups; Lee, Kate, Dayle and Karen in
Room 6, everyone at Tendring Community Writers and to everyone in my
Writeretreatuk writing group.

To Ken Worpole and Travis Elborough for kind words. My publisher
and friend Eleanor Vonne Brown at Publishing Household for sound
advice, encouragement and enthusiasm, to Lily Bates for editorial
assistance, and Claire Mason (Flushleft) for design inspiration.
And finally, to Ada my grandmother, my connection to Frinton and
Walton, and the name of my imagined beach hut.

ABOUT THE AUTHOR

Nancy Stevenson is a writer and researcher. Her research centres on people's engagement in leisure activities and is embedded in local landscapes. She has written about festivals, walking, writing and wellbeing and the importance of pleasure and play in community life. She spends her time between North London and the Essex Coast, and hosts writing retreats in Frinton-on-Sea. *Beach Hut People* is her first book.

[instagram] @write_nancy_write
www.writeretreatuk.org